TIMESAVER **FOR EXAM**

IELTS Writing

(5.5–7.5)

By Verity Cole

Contents

Introduction

Who is this book for?

This book is for teachers of students preparing for the Academic version of the IELTS test, and who are aiming for a score of 5.5 – 7.5. It is an ideal supplement to any IELTS preparation coursebook, especially for students who already have a good grounding in English. The topics and activities reflect those typical of the IELTS Academic test and are designed especially to appeal to young adults. This resource is also suitable for use with any upper-intermediate or advanced classes who wish to begin to develop their academic writing, especially with a view to academic study.

The IELTS test: an overview

The International English Language Testing System (IELTS) is a test that measures the language proficiency of people who want to study or work in environments where English is used as a language of communication. An easy-to-use 9-band scale clearly identifies proficiency level, from non-user (band score 1) through to expert (band score 9).

IELTS is available in two test formats – Academic or General Training – and provides a valid and accurate assessment of the four language skills: listening, reading, writing and speaking. This Timesaver title focuses on the Academic version of the test.

There are four components to the test.

Reading 60 minutes.
There are three texts with 40 questions.

Writing 60 minutes.
There are two writing tasks. Task 1 has a minimum of 150 words. Task 2 has a minimum of 250 words.

Listening 30 minutes (plus 10 minutes for transferring answers).
There are four sections with 40 questions.

Speaking 11-14 minutes.
There are three parts.

Scoring
Each component of the test is given a band score. The average of the four scores produces the overall band score. You do not pass or fail IELTS; you receive a score.

The IELTS scale

BAND SCORE	SKILL LEVEL	DESCRIPTION
9	Expert user	The test taker has fully operational command of the language. Their use of English is appropriate, accurate and fluent, and shows complete understanding.
8	Very good user	The test taker has fully operational command of the language with only occasional unsystematic inaccuracies and inappropriate usage. They may misunderstand some things in unfamiliar situations. They handle complex and detailed argumentation well.
7	Good user	The test taker has operational command of the language, though with occasional inaccuracies, inappropriate usage and misunderstandings in some situations. They generally handle complex language well and understand detailed reasoning.
6	Competent user	The test taker has an effective command of the language despite some inaccuracies, inappropriate usage and misunderstandings. They can use and understand fairly complex language, particularly in familiar situations.
5	Modest user	The test taker has a partial command of the language and copes with overall meaning in most situations, although they are likely to make many mistakes. They should be able to handle basic communication in their own field.
4	Limited user	The test taker's basic competence is limited to familiar situations. They frequently show problems in understanding and expression. They are not able to use complex language.
3	Extremely limited user	The test taker conveys and understands only general meaning in very familiar situations. There are frequent breakdowns in communication.
2	Intermittent user	The test taker has great difficulty understanding spoken and written English.
1	Non-user	The test taker has no ability to use the language except a few isolated words.

For full details on the IELTS test, go to: **www.ielts.org**

How do I use this book?

The book is divided into thirteen pairs of lessons. The first lesson in each pair covers Task 1 and the second Task 2 of the IELTS Academic writing component. Both lessons are based around a theme which IELTS candidates may be required to write about. Use the lessons to supplement your coursebook by providing extra practice of particular parts of the test or topic areas. The activities also provide thorough practice of exam skills.

- The activities are designed to be teacher-led but are used without separate Teacher's notes. Clear instructions are on the pages, which are all photocopiable.

- The test section, question type and lesson focus are clearly labelled in each lesson.

- The lessons have been designed to cover one hour of class time, depending on class size and language level.

- The comprehensive answer key at the back of the book provides an explanation of the answers. It also provides example answers for each of the exam tasks and the test questions.

- There are writing tips in each lesson to raise students' awareness of the most important strategies for academic writing.

- Some activities ask students to work in pairs or groups to maximise their engagement with the writing skills and language. These can be adapted depending on context and class size.

- There is an exam task in every lesson, which requires students to write a complete essay. These tasks are ideal to set as homework, or as timed writing practice under exam conditions in class.

- The activities are followed by an IELTS Writing practice test. Sample answers are provided with examiner commentary at two different levels. An official answer sheet is provided for the Writing Task 1 (the Task 2 sheet is identical in format).

How important are writing skills to exam success?

The IELTS test requires candidates to be able to use a wide range of writing skills. In Task 1, candidates may be required to describe data presented in one or more graphs, charts or tables. Alternatively, they may have to describe a diagram of a machine, a device or a process and be asked to explain how it works. They may also be required to describe a map and to either evaluate the suitability of two possible development sites or to describe changes that have occurred in a place over time. Candidates will need to demonstrate an ability to identify the most important and relevant information and to organise their answer well, using language accurately in an academic style. In Task 2, candidates are asked to write a discursive essay about a given topic and are required to write a response which is fully relevant to the specific question set. This task evaluates the candidate's ability to present a clear argument, which is relevant and well-organised.

The activities in this book develop the candidates' ability to master each of the Task 1 and Task 2 question types in turn and help students to structure answers logically, use language appropriately in order to attain a higher band score and deal with difficult questions. As well as this, exam tips alert students to ways of avoiding common pitfalls. Example answers are provided for candidates to analyse and to use as a guide. There is also a sample answer for each of the exam tasks in the Answer Key at the back of the book.

To achieve a score of 5.5 to 7.5 in the IELTS Writing Test, candidates need to be able to organise ideas following an appropriate structure, and they need to write in an appropriate academic style. In Task 2, they also need to demonstrate an ability to reason and evaluate. They should use a wide range of vocabulary which is accurate and relevant to the topic and use suitable grammar to convey concepts accurately and to link ideas. At this level they are expected to handle complex language well, with the occasional mistake. The lessons in this book offer extensive guidance and practice opportunities for structuring answers and for writing in an appropriate style. They also practise useful vocabulary connected with common IELTS topics, and practise grammar which is useful for various basic functions in academic writing, such as describing trends or expressing cause and effect relationships.

The Timesaver series

The Timesaver series provides hundreds of ready-made lessons for all language levels and age groups, covering skills work, language practice and cross-curricular and cross-cultural material. See the full range of print and digital resources at: **www.scholastic.co.uk/elt**

English as an additional language

1a **Work in pairs. Which of the ten countries in the box do you think have the highest numbers of people who speak English as an additional language? Put the countries in order from highest to lowest.**

> Bangladesh China Egypt France Germany India Nigeria Pakistan Philippines United States

1b **Check your guesses from exercise 1 in the answer key. Did anything surprise you? How do you think your country compares to others in terms of numbers of English speakers?**

2a **Look at the bar graph and answer the questions.**

1 Can you describe what the bar graph shows in your own words, using the title of the graph to help you?

2 Does the graph include data from one specific point in time or data from a period of time?

3 Are the quantities in the graph in the form of numbers or percentages?

4 What tense should you use in a written description of the graph?

5 What important data in the graph would you select to describe?

6 How would you group data in the graph into paragraphs in a written description?

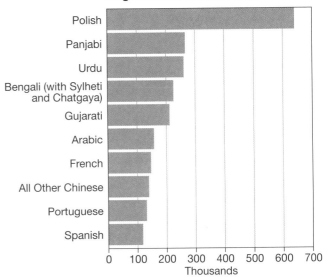

Top ten main 'other' languages in England and Wales in 2011

2b **Read the description of the bar chart. Has the writer made the same decisions as you in questions 3–5 of exercise 2a?**

The bar graph compares the number of people who had a main language other than English who were residents of England and Wales in 2011.

From the graph, we can see that Polish was spoken by the **1** .... (high) number of people, with around 550,000 people reporting it as their main language. After Polish, the next **2** .... (common) main languages were from South Asia. Approximately 270,000 people living in England and Wales spoke Panjabi and only **slightly 3** .... (few) had Urdu as their main language. The numbers of Bengali and Gujarati speakers were **4** .... (low), at around 220 and 215 thousand respectively. Overall, there were **far 5** .... (few) speakers of Chinese languages, however — only 140,000 people, **compared to around double the number** of Panjabi speakers.

The language spoken by the **6** .... (few) people in the UK and Wales was Spanish, with only 120,000 people reporting it as their main language. The number of speakers of other European languages were only **marginally 7** .... (high), with around 230,000 people speaking Portuguese as their main language and 235,000 speaking French. The number of speakers of Arabic were **comparable to** those of French.

> **Exam tip**
>
> When you are comparing data, it is a good idea to select and group data into paragraphs. Your description should start with the most important or noticeable piece of data in the graph.

2c Complete the description in exercise 2b with the correct comparative or superlative form of the word in brackets.

2d Which word(s) in bold in the description:

a) describe a small difference? b) describe a big difference?

c) describes a similarity? d) means the same as 'approximately twice as many'?

3a It is important to avoid repeating words unnecessarily in Writing Task 1. Read the two short paragraphs. Which one avoids repetition? How does the writer use 'respectively'?

> **A** *Approximately 270,000 people living in England and Wales spoke Panjabi and only slightly fewer people living in England and Wales had Urdu as their main language. The numbers of Bengali and Gujarati speakers were lower. There were around 220 thousand Bengali speakers and 215 thousand Gujarati speakers.*
>
> **B** *Approximately 270,000 people living in England and Wales spoke Panjabi and only slightly fewer had Urdu as their main language. The numbers of Bengali and Gujarati speakers were lower at around 220 and 215 thousand respectively.*

3b Make changes to this extract from a Writing Task 1 answer so that it avoids unnecessary repetition.

Overall, we can see that the highest number of proficient Spanish speakers arrived in the US between 2004 and 2009. We can also see that during this time, there were far higher numbers of advanced Spanish speakers from Spain than there were Spanish speakers from Mexico. Between 2004 and 2006, and between 2007 and 2009, there were 216,000 Spanish speakers from Spain and nearly 150,000 more proficient Spanish speakers from Spain.

✏ EXAM TASK

4a Work in pairs. Look at the graph below. Discuss questions 1–6 in exercise 2a again.

4b The graph shows the number of proficient English speakers from different countries by the year of their arrival in England and Wales. Summarise the information by selecting and reporting the main features, and make comparisons where relevant. Write at least 150 words.

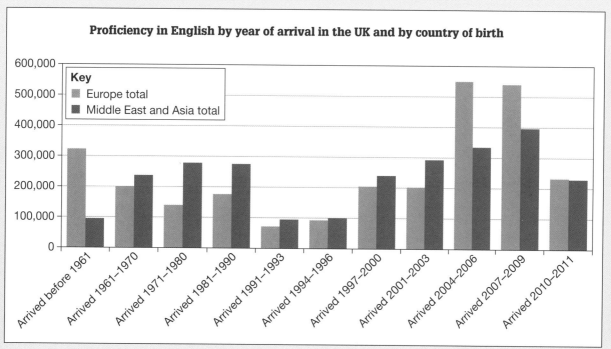

Saving languages

1a **Read the text about Tom and endangered languages. What do the numbers in the box refer to?**

| 3,000 | 6,000 | 10 | 50% |

Tom Belt, a native of Oklahoma, USA, is one of few people in the world who speaks Cherokee, a language that is thought to originate from the Great Lakes area of North America around 3,000 years ago. When Tom learned that Cherokee was on the brink of extinction, he decided to do something to save it. He volunteered to teach Cherokee lessons at a local school and now teaches the language at a local university. Cherokee is far from the only endangered language, however. According to linguists, around half of the world's remaining 6000 languages are imperilled and are likely to become extinct by the end of this century. Today, the 'top ten' languages in the world are spoken by 50% of the world's population.

1b **Work in pairs. What do you think? In pairs, discuss the questions.**

a) Are we going to become a monolingual species, and if so, is this a good thing?

b) Should we be doing more to save the world's endangered languages?.

1c **Read the Writing Task 2 questions below. Match them to the questions in exercise 1b.**

A | Several languages around the world are in danger of dying out because they are spoken by very few people. Some people say that governments should spend public money on saving these languages, while others believe that would be a waste of money.
Discuss both these views and give your opinion.

B | Due to the development of tourism, English has become the most widely used and best-known language in the world. Some people think that this will result in English becoming the only language to be spoken globally.
What are the advantages and disadvantages to having one language in the world?

1d **Work in pairs. Discuss which of the tasks asks the writer to …**

a) discuss benefits and drawbacks.   **b)** express their views on both sides of an argument.

2a **Planning your essay allows you to organise your ideas and develop your arguments fully. In your pairs, look at the essay plans for question B below. Which way of planning would help you to:**

a) think of lots of different ideas and vocabulary, without worrying about structure?

b) develop a balanced argument?

c) think of examples and explanations to support your points?

A

PHOTOCOPIABLE

B

Advantages	Disadvantages
.... makes tourism easier: everyone can understand one another.	.... leads to a lack of understanding of the arts: great works such as the iliad were not written down until very recently. some that are never written down might be lost forever.
.... enables everyone to access and understand diverse cultures: literary works from different cultures translated into a single language.	.... leads to a loss of knowledge about a place: e.g. amazonian languages tell us about the rainforest.
.... facilitates globalisation: business is easier and cheaper to do with a common language.	.... leads to loss of cultural identity: language defines a particular people and their sense of self.
.... cheaper: translation becomes unnecessary.	.... leads to loss of particular words: some words are particular to a language e.g. oo-kah-huh-sdee (cherokee) (cute, gorgeous, delight, engendering a desire to squeeze something – the feeling when you see a kitten).

2b Read the sample essay below. Number the ideas in plan B above in the order that they appear in the essay. Which idea is not used?

Many people believe it is inevitable that English will become the exclusive language of communication and, therefore other languages will become extinct. There are both benefits and drawbacks to a single global language.

In a number of ways, communicating in a single language is more convenient. Colleagues who have English as a second language can communicate considerably more easily. Since translation is not necessarily, companies can also save a great deal of money.

Outside the world of work, a single language is also useful. It removes difficulties when people travel. For instance, shopping becomes simpler. 'Couch tourists' can also benefit from a single language. If all literary works are translated into English, readers can readily explore different cultures.

However, there is a considerable price to pay for the use of a single language. That is the loss of a people's cultural identity. Language features words and ideas which are unique to a culture. For example, in Cherokee, there is no word for goodbye. Instead they say 'I will see you again.' Extinction of a language also means that particular words die. If Indonesian wasn't spoken any more, no one would learn the world Jayus (A joke so poorly told and so unfunny that one cannot help but laugh). As a result, languages become impoverished.

There is also the argument that when a language dies, vital knowledge about an area dies with it. There are many endangered languages spoken by Amazonian people in the rainforest. If these are lost, an understanding of the rainforest environment also disappears forever.

In conclusion, although communication in a single, global language is convenient and economical, I would argue for the preservation of endangered languages in order to avoid loss of cultural identity and important knowledge and to ensure that language remains interesting and diverse.

Exam tip

Use different words to those in the question in the introduction to your essay. It shows that you have a wide vocabulary.

2c Read the introduction to the essay again. Find words in the introduction which have a similar meaning to words in task A in exercise 1c.

2d Which words and phrases does the writer use that are connected to 'convenience' and 'loss'? Complete the table with words from the essay.

✎ EXAM TASK

3 Look at task A in exercise 1c again. Write your essay. Give reasons for your answer and include any relevant examples from your own knowledge and experience. Write at least 250 words.

Location is everything

1a Work in pairs. Draw a simple map of your school and the surrounding area. Mark the compass directions (north, south, east and west) on your map.

1b In your pairs, take turns to describe the location of five different places in relation to your school. Your partner should guess the place. Use the phrases in the box to help.

> outside the town   to the north / east / south / west of the school   in the countryside
> a few kilometres away from the school   equidistant between … and …
> in the north / east / south / west of the city   in the suburbs   in the town centre   close to …
> nearby   opposite   on the main road   on the railway line

2a Work in pairs. Look at the map of the city of Cambrook and the surrounding area. Describe the two possible locations for the cinema and leisure complex firstly in relation to the city and secondly in relation to transport links. Then decide which is the best location for the new complex. Give reasons for your answer.

> The map below is of the city of Cambrook. A new cinema and leisure complex (S) is planned for the town. The map shows two possible sites for the complex.

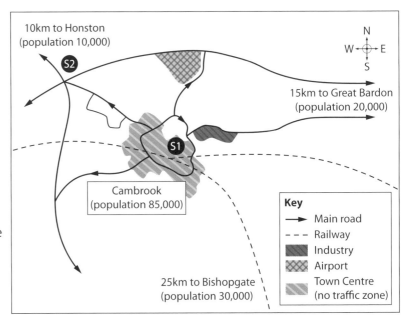

10km to Honston (population 10,000)
S2
N
W E
S
15km to Great Bardon (population 20,000)
S1
Cambrook (population 85,000)
25km to Bishopgate (population 30,000)

Key
→ Main road
--- Railway
▨ Industry
▧ Airport
▨ Town Centre (no traffic zone)

2b Read the sample map description and insert the correct sentence or phrase (A–D) in the gaps.

1 If the leisure complex was situated in S1, it would be easily accessible for the 85,000 Cambrook residents,

2 With regard to convenience for residents of the villages outside Cambrook,

3 The map illustrates two potential locations for a new cinema and leisure development.

4 Although the location of both S1 and S2 have advantages and disadvantages,

A .... One possible site is in the city centre (S1), which is a no traffic zone, and the other is to the north-west of the city centre (S2).

B .... whereas if it was out of town, they would have to travel. On the other hand, Cambrook residents may not appreciate the increased traffic congestion that a leisure complex in town would create.

C .... S2 is well-situated for the 10,000 people living in Honston and in Great Bardon, who could reach the complex by car or bus. Conversely, it is not so easy for these people to get into Cambrook, particularly because the complex at S1 would be located in a pedestrian zone, making parking difficult. However, S2 is not easily accessible for Bishopgate, as there isn't a main road from this town towards it. Because of the proximity of S1 to a railway line and the fact that the line passes through Bishopgate, its residents would probably prefer S1.

D .... I would recommend that the leisure centre is located at S2, due to the fact that it would be accessible to residents of Cambrook, Honston and Great Bardon, without contributing to traffic congestion.

2c **Read the model answer above again and <u>underline</u>:**

a) 3 linking words and one phrase that contrasts information that goes before it with information after it

b) 4 clauses that give reasons why a location is convenient or not

c) 4 relative clauses and one present participle clause that adds extra information to a sentence

2d **Complete the sample answer that describes two possible locations for a supermarket by choosing the correct answer.**

If the supermarket was built on the first proposed site, it would necessitate the clearing of an area of land and the cutting down of trees, **(1)** *which would / because* cause some environmental damage. **(2)** *As / Conversely*, it wouldn't cause traffic congestion, **(3)** *because it is situated / whilst it is situated away from an already built-up area*. **(4)** *As / On the other hand*, the second site is likely to suffer from this problem and may lead to the city centre becoming more polluted.

In terms of accessibility, the second site is undoubtedly more convenient for the residents of the majority of the housing zone, apart from those living in the north western area, **(5)** *which / who* would benefit from the first location.

> **Exam tip**
>
> Don't write a separate paragraph about each location: it's much better to compare and contrast the sites. For example, in one paragraph, you could compare the sites in relation to the main city and in the other paragraph, you could compare the sites in relation to transport links and surrounding towns.

✏ EXAM TASK

3a **Work in pairs. Look at the exam task below. Discuss how you would organise your description of the two possible locations shown.**

3b **Think of words that you could use in your map introduction instead of the <u>underlined</u> words in the exam question.**

The map below is of the city of Long Melling. A new <u>shopping centre</u> (S) is planned for the town. The map shows two <u>possible sites</u> for the centre. Summarise the information by selecting and reporting the main features, and making comparisons where relevant.

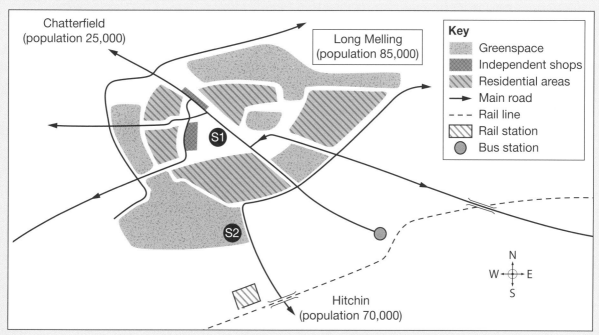

3c **Write your description. Write at least 150 words.**

The wrong move?

1a Discuss in pairs. What are the advantages and disadvantages of living in a city compared to living in the countryside?

1b Choose the words in the box which apply to each picture (A or B).

> 'concrete jungles'   air pollution   developed infrastructure   good education resources   high cost of living
> homelessness and poverty   higher stress levels   laid-back, slow pace of life   limited career prospects
> modern transportation links   overpopulation   peaceful   sense of anonymity   sparsely populated
> tightly-knit communities   traffic congestion   locally cultivated, organic food

2 Read the Writing Task 2 questions. Decide which type of questions they are.

a) problem solution   **b**) opinion   **c**) cause and result

> **1** More and more people are re-locating to cities, but city life can be very challenging. Describe some of the difficulties of living in a city. How can governments improve urban life for everyone?

> **2** The growing housing problem in big cities has social consequences. Many people feel that it is the responsibility of the government to solve this problem. To what extent do you agree or disagree?

3a Read the first line of an essay introduction for question 1 in exercise 2. The writer has repeated words from the task question in the introduction. Replace these words with words from the box.

> an increasing number of   has a number of drawbacks
> issues   metropolitan living   move

Nowadays, more and more people are choosing to re-locate to cities. However, living in cities can be very challenging. There are many difficulties associated with urban life. For example, …

Exam tip

In essay introductions, show that you have a good range of language by paraphrasing the words that are used in the test question.

3b Work in pairs. Read these three essay introductions for question 2 in exercise 2. Discuss which you think is the most successful. Give reasons for your answer.

a) These days, the increasing number of people choosing to reside in cities has created a number of social issues. For example, a housing and land shortage often means that prices of residences are pushed up, resulting in low earners being unable to afford to buy a home and therefore having to pay exorbitant rents or commute into the city, which, in turn, leads to traffic congestion. Without doubt, it is the duty of the government to address these issues. Only the government has the power to change laws so that more land is made available for housing. Equally, it is the government, in the UK, who decides whether to build more social housing, for those who can't afford to buy. In addition, the government can introduce legislation which bans the rich from purchasing second homes and they can also build more retirement properties, to encourage the elderly to downsize from family-size homes. Admittedly, the government cannot stipulate that developers build more affordable homes, but as I've outlined above, they can take steps to reduce the pressure on current housing provision.

b) These days, the increasing number of people choosing to reside in cities has created a number of social issues. For instance, the greater demand for houses and the shortage of land to build more residences has led to a rise in house prices. This means that while high earners can afford to buy in cities, people on lower wages cannot afford to buy a house and therefore have to pay very high rents, or live in sub-standard housing that they can afford. In my view, this is a very regrettable situation. I don't feel it is right that there is such an inequality in the standard of living. This essay will explore the reasons why both high and low earners should be able to afford to buy a house.

c) These days, the increasing number of people choosing to reside in cities has created social inequality. For example, the rising price of houses created by a lack of housing and land has resulted in only high earners being able to buy in the city. In my opinion, the onus of solving this disparity in living standards is on the government. This essay will explore reasons why the government should address the social issues caused by a lack of housing.

3c **Match the teacher's comments to each of the essay introductions in exercise 3b.**

1 Good effort. You've paraphrased the words in the questions, you've given examples of a social issue and you've made your opinion clear. The reader will also have a good idea of what to expect from the rest of your essay.

2 This is very detailed. Perhaps too detailed! You've answered the whole question in your introduction. I'm worried you're not going to have enough to say in the rest of your essay. Try just to introduce the topic and indicate your opinion.

3 This starts well, but I think you've gone off-topic a little. You seem to be expressing your opinion on the gravity of the social issues brought about by the housing crisis, rather than on whether you agree that solving the housing shortage is the government's responsibility. Make sure you answer the question.

4a **Read the advice below. Look back at the essay introductions in exercise 3b. How does each writer express their opinion?**

1 an example that explains the issue outlined in the question in more detail

2 an indication of your opinion in response to the question asked. This doesn't have to be one-sided. It's acceptable to say that you have mixed views.

3 the reader an idea of what to expect in the rest of the essay.

4b **Find synonyms for each of these words in the essay introductions.**

a) reside (verb) **b)** residences (noun) **c)** a rise (verb) **d)** people on low wages

e) a duty **f)** pass laws **g)** affordable **h)** a supply

i) inequality **j)** to tackle **k)** a crisis **l)** a shortage

---

✏ EXAM TASK

5a **Work in pairs. Read the IELTS test question below. Plan the points that you will include in your introduction.**

> Traffic and housing problems in large cities could be addressed by moving large companies and factories and their employees to the countryside.
>
> To what extent do you agree or disagree with this opinion?

Give reasons for your answer and include any relevant examples from your own knowledge or experience. Write at least 250 words.

5b **Write an introduction in response to the essay question.**

How much sleep do you need?

1 **Work in pairs. Discuss the questions.**

a) How many hours sleep do you get on average per night?

b) Does the amount of sleep you get differ between weeknights and weekends?

c) Look at the illustration of daily sleep needs by age. Do you and your family get enough sleep per night? If not, why not?

d) How do you think a lack of sleep affects your studies / work?

e) How do you cope with sleep deprivation when you're at school / work?

| Newborn 12 to 18 hrs. | Infants 14 to 15 hrs. | Preschoolers 11 to 13 hrs. | Schoolchildren 10 to 11 hrs. | Teens 8.5 to 9.5 hrs. | Adults 7 to 9 hrs. |

2a **Look at the table. Complete the sentences that describe the data in the table.**

1 The graph illustrates the changes to students' grades brought about by Jackson Hole High School starting 90 minutes later in .... than in ....

2 Overall, we can see a slight increase in GPA (grade point average) across all .... grades, or year groups.

3 The grade that saw the highest point increase was grade ...., with an increase of .71 points, while the grade that saw the lowest rise was grade .... which improved by .33 points.

EFFECT OF LATER SCHOOL START TIME ON STUDENT GPA

Jackson Hole High School in Wyoming switched to a later start time in the 2012-13 school year. Here's how the change affected students' GPA by grade.

GRADE	Average GPA with 7.35 a.m. start time (2011-12)	Average GPA with 7.35 a.m. start time (2011-12)
9	2.62	3.10
10	2.62	3.33
11	2.72	3.05
12	2.53	3.04

SOURCE WAHLSTROM ET ALL, 2014

2b **Discuss in pairs. Why do you think a change in school start time affected the students' grades?**

2c **What is the function of sentences 2 and 3 in exercise 2a?**

a) to describe a detail in the table.

b) to describe a general data trend in the table

c) to draw attention to the most significant pieces of information in the table.

Exam tip

When describing a graph, start by explaining what the graph shows, then give an overview or summary of the most noticeable trends in the graph.

3a **Look at the graph below. Answer the questions.**

a) Overall, what does the data suggest about the sleep habits of adolescents and young adults between 2004 and 2013?

b) What do the numbers on the top of the vertical axis represent: number of students or percentages?

c) Which tense would you use to describe the trends in the line graph?

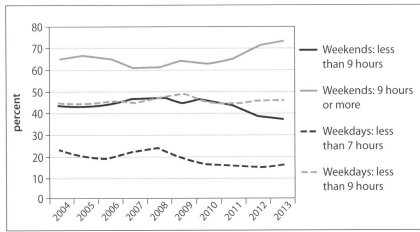

3b **Read the sample description of the graph. In which of these ways has the writer grouped the data?**

a) by number of hours' sleep

b) by weekends and weekdays

The graph illustrates the changes in sleep duration experienced by young adults in the years between 2004 and 2013.

In general, we can see that sleep duration was highest at weekends, and the percentage of young adults accruing more than nine hours of sleep increased markedly between 2007 and 2013. In addition, we can also see that the overall percentage of sleep duration increased.

Although the percentage of young adults getting less than 9 hours' sleep on weekdays remained relatively consistent, with slight fluctuations, those adults reporting fewer than seven hours' sleep on weekdays fell dramatically from a peak of 24.5 percent in 2008 to a low of 14.8 in 2012, before increasing marginally again in 2013.

There was a steady rise in weekend sleep duration to a high in 2008 of 39% of young adults who were getting less than 7 hours sleep per night. However, there was then a significant decrease in percentage between 2010 and 2013, of around 11%. There was a concurrent rise in the percentage of adults getting more than nine hours' sleep over the same period.

3c <u>Underline</u> the following in the sample description:

1 adjectives that moderate nouns describing change

2 adverbs that moderate verbs describing change

3 an adverb that moderates an adjective describing change

3d **Discuss in pairs. Which of the adjectives and adverbs that you underlined describe a big change? Which describe a small change?**

Look back at the sample description in exercise 3b. When increase / decrease is used as a noun, how is the sentence usually started?.

✏ EXAM TASK

4a **Work in pairs. Read the exam task and plan your graph description.**

The line graph below shows the percentage of adolescents ages 15 to 19 who report getting different amounts of sleep on the previous night, 2003–2012. Summarise the information by selecting and reporting the main features, and make comparisons where relevant.

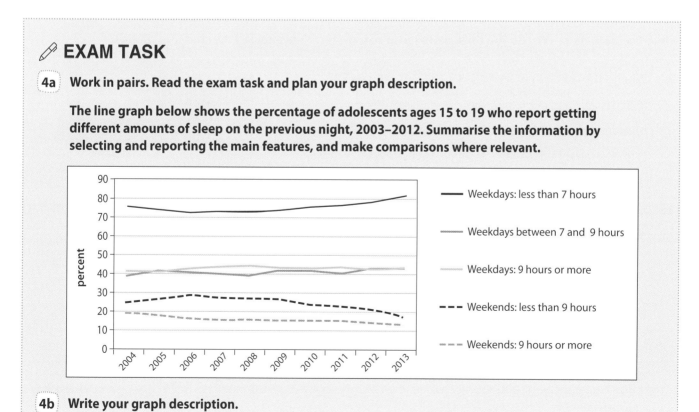

4b **Write your graph description.**

60 mins

Education matters

1a **Work in pairs. Read the newspaper extracts about problems in the UK education sector. Discuss the questions.**

a) Why do you think these problems have come about?

b) What is likely to be the consequences of these issues?

c) Do educational institutions in your country face similar challenges?

1
Fewer young people studying STEM

A recent, government-funded report has found that for the last ten years there has been a decline in the number of secondary-school pupils studying the STEM (science, technology, engineering and mathematics) subjects, which is creating a shortage of young people embarking in technology and engineering careers.

2
Government warns of rising university tuition fees

The minister of education has recently announced that university tuition fees are likely to rise again next year, in line with an increase in inflation. Universities have broadly supported this decision, arguing that it will allow them to uphold high standards of teaching.

3
Apprenticeships have an image problem as students prefer higher education

New research suggests that apprenticeships have an image problem among young people in the UK. The research finds that they are five times less likely than people over the age of 50 to see any value in taking a vocational path into a career.

1b **Match the topics of the newspaper extracts to the essay questions.**

1 Some people believe that governments should pay for education, but others disagree with this opinion. Discuss both views and give your own opinion.

2 Many people consider a university degree essential to having a successful future career, whereas others maintain that it is better to apply for a job after leaving school.
Discuss both views and give your opinion.

3 Some people feel that it is more important for students to study history, literature and art than it is for them to study science and mathematics. Discuss both views and give your opinion.

1c **Work in groups of three. Think of three points to support each view for each of the essay tasks.**

PHOTOCOPIABLE

1d A topic sentence introduces the main idea to be discussed in a paragraph. Which of these topic sentences is too general, too specific or just right?

1 If governments do not fund higher education, students from disadvantaged backgrounds are unlikely to be able to attend university.

2 A university education is expensive.

3 A lack of government funding mean that access to education is limited for some.

2a The sentences in each of the two paragraphs below are not in the correct order. Number them in the correct order. Then underline the topic sentence. Circle the linking words.

Paragraph 1

a) At present, the government gives financial benefits to the unemployed and disadvantaged, which is a huge drain on taxpayers' resources. ....

b) Consequently, there would be less need for unemployment benefit to be paid. ....

c) Equal access to free education for all would benefit society as a whole. ....

d) If the government instead subsidised university places to ensure that pupils from all economic backgrounds could attend, this would lead to a higher rate of employment in the future. ....

Paragraph 2

a) Not only is this likely to be more interesting and offer more potential for professional development than those jobs available to school leavers, but it is also bound to be better paid. ....

b) On the other hand, the individual paying for a higher education could be viewed as a necessary investment which, in turn, opens up opportunities. ....

c) Therefore, it is probable that a parents' initial investment will be repaid in the long run. ....

d) Those families who decide to pay for a university education for their son and daughter are increasing the likelihood of them securing a graduate level job in the future. ....

> **Exam tip**
>
> To make your essay easier to read, use a topic sentence at the beginning of a paragraph. Be careful not to make your topic sentences too general or too specific.

2b Which of these words and phrases have similar meanings to linking words you've circled?

a) also **b)** as a result **c)** however **d)** rather, **e)** then **f)** thus

2c Circle the correct linking words to complete the paragraph below.

A lack of government funding mean that access to education is limited for some. Students from economically disadvantaged families, for example, are very unlikely to be able to afford to go to university. **(1)** *As a result / Also* students who may be academically gifted do not have the opportunity to fulfil their potential and are, **(2)** *on the other hand / instead* limited to dead-end jobs. **(3)** *Not only / Also* does the allocation of university places on a financial basis seem unjust, **(4)** *however / but* it also means that society is not benefitting from some bright young minds.

✎ EXAM TASK

3a Work in pairs. Plan your response to essay question 3 in exercise 1b. Try to think of a general topic sentence for each paragraph.

3b Write your essay in around 250 words.

The age-wage gap

1a **Work in pairs. Discuss which of these statements are true or false for your country.**

a) The older a person is, the more they tend to earn.

b) The highest earners are generally between 18 and 21 years' old.

c) On the whole, young male graduates earn more than young female graduates.

d) Peak earning age is when a person is in their 40s.

e) Times are tough for young people. They earn a low wage but the cost of living is increasing.

1b **Discuss whether you feel it's fair for people of different ages who work in the same company to earn different amounts. Give reasons for your answers.**

2a **Look at the table below. Answer the questions.**

a) What does the table show?

b) In terms of age of employee, what overall trend can you see?

c) Between what ages can you see the greatest differences in earnings?

d) Does this differ between full-time and part-time employees?

e) In terms of gender, what overall trend can you see?

f) Can you see any exceptions to this trend?

Median weekly gross income of employees in the UK, in 2015 (£)				
Age of employee	Female full-time employees	Male full-time employees	Female part-time employees	Male part-time employees
16–17	147.7	171.60	48	54.8
18–21	293.20	314.10	97.7	103.2
22–29	422.10	443.60	154.20	158.1
20–39	538.20	584.80	191.40	179.30
40–49	521.70	653.40	192.70	180
50–59	475.7	630.0	188.50	187.1
60+	421.9	541.10	154.40	166.7

g) Between what ages can you see the greatest differences in earnings between the genders?

2b **Read a sample answer that describes the table. Check your answers to exercise 2a.**

A The table shows the median wage per week in 2015 of employees of different types.

B In general, we can see that, for both full-time and part-time employees in 2015, salaries were lowest at ages 16–17, and peaked when the employee reached 20–39 for full-time employees, and 40–49 for part-time employees. After these ages, earning capacity got lower, with both full-time male and female employees of 60 years plus earning around £100 per week less than an employee of 40 to 50 years old.

C If we compare genders, we can see that male employees earned much more than female employees earned. The greatest gap in wages for full-time employees was between male and female workers of between 50 and 59. In contrast, the wage difference was greater for part-time employees earlier on, between the ages of 16 and 17. The wage difference was greater between the ages of 16 and 17. It was also much less; at about £7 per week.

D We can see an exception to the gender wage gap in part-time workers. In contrast to their full time female employees, from the age of 20 to 60, female part-time employees actually earned more than male part-time employees.

2c **Work in pairs. Discuss the answers to these questions.**

Has the candidate who wrote the sample answer in exercise 2b:

a) included all of the most important information? **b)** grouped the information in a logical way?

c) used a wide variety of language? **d)** repeated vocabulary or structures unnecessarily?

3a Look at paragraph C. Are there any words or phrases that could be deleted? Could you replace any repeated words or phrases with a pronoun?

3b Replace repeated words and phrases in paragraphs A–D with the alternatives in the box. You will need to use a passive structure in paragraph D.

> brought home   by contrast   can be observed   considerably   counterparts   overall
> part-timers   salary   significantly   wage earner   we can notice that   worker

3c After you have written the first draft of your table description, consider the following questions:

Have I used:

- a mixture of passive and active structures?
- a range of adverbs to modify adjectives?
- verbs or adjectives instead of nouns

✏ EXAM TASK

4 Work in pairs. Your teacher will tell you if you're pair A or pair B. Follow the correct instruction.

PAIR A

a) The table shows the median annual gross income of employees in different countries in 2015 in dollars. Summarise the information by selecting and reporting the main features, and make comparisons where relevant. Write at least 150 words.

b) Show the first draft of your table description to Pair B. Ask them to check your draft for repetition and range of language.

c) Compare the data in your table with the data in Pair B's table. What overall trends can you spot for the countries listed?

Median annual gross income of employees in different countries, in 2015 ($)		
Country	Female full-time employees	Male full-time employees
Philippines	5,643	8,184
Norway	57, 293	72, 471
Qatar	59, 334	164,771
Sweden	39,996	50, 323
Vietnam	5, 108	6,162
Lithuania	23,011	30,901
China	10,037	16,170
UAE	23, 688	80,745

PAIR B

a) The table shows senior and management positions held by female and male employees in different countries in 2015. Summarise the information by selecting and reporting the main features, and make comparisons where relevant. Write at least 150 words.

b) Show the first draft of your table description to Pair A. Ask them to check your draft for repetition and range of language.

c) Compare the data in your table with the data in Pair B's table. What overall trends can you spot for the countries listed?

Senior and management positions held, in 2015 (%)		
Country	Female full-time employees	Male full-time employees
Philippines	57	43
Norway	36	64
Qatar	12	88
Sweden	37	63
Vietnam	24	76
Lithuania	39	61
China	17	83
UAE	10	90

60 mins

Stiff competition

1   Discuss in pairs. Look at the job applicant profiles. If you were an employer, which person would you give an engineering job to? Give reasons for your answer.

NAME: David

AGE: 55

EXPERIENCE: Worked as mechanical engineer for one firm for 25 years

NAME: Peter

AGE: 19

EXPERIENCE: Recent engineering graduate. Completed a work-placement at UK-based engineering company while at university.

2   Which of these phrases would you associate with:

a) a younger employee?   **b)** an older employee?

> a need to be trained up   ambitious and single-minded   brings a sense of perspective
> committed to accuracy   conversant with new technologies   dependable and punctual
> expensive to make redundant   generous with their time and expertise   highly qualified   innovative and
> willing to take risks   a lack of work experience   more flexible with their time

3a   Read the essay title. If you had to choose to either agree or disagree, which would you choose?

> Companies should encourage senior employees to leave at the age of 55 in order to give opportunities to young job seekers.
>
> To what extent do you agree or disagree with this opinion?

3b   Read the two introductory paragraphs and answer the questions. Which paragraph(s)

a) uses informal quantifiers and intensifying adverbs (e.g. really)?

b) expresses viewpoints in the first person (i.e. I)?

c) uses punctuation marks to express opinion and poses rhetorical questions?

d) uses formal linking words?

e) avoids using the first person by using it structures (it is believed that) and there structures + adjectives (There are good reasons)?

f) tentatively makes claims (e.g. suggest)?

g) uses informal vocabulary?

3c   Which paragraph do you feel is more suitable for an academic IELTS essay?

A Lots of young people feel that older people should retire so that they have the chance to get a job. Personally speaking, I completely agree with this. These days, loads of young people are finding it really hard to get a job and their talents and expensive qualifications are being totally wasted. Why should old people, who've already enjoyed a full career, continue to keep all the plum jobs? It's outrageous!

B It is a widely held opinion that experienced employees of 40 years or older are responsible for the scarcity of positions that are available for younger people. Therefore, many people feel that older employees should retire to make way for young graduates. There are, however, a number of compelling arguments that suggest that older employees in the workplace actually benefit young job applicants, both in terms of the boost they give to the economy and because of the experience they are willing to share. This essay explores these advantages.

4a **Work in pairs. Think of arguments against these points.**

a) Many people feel that encouraging older workers to stay in the labour force will take away jobs from the young.

b) It is claimed that older workers are far more expensive to retain than younger employees.

c) It is a generally held belief that younger employees are more innovative, have better IT skills and are more able bodied, so more capable of the rigours of work.

> **Exam tip**
>
> You can write in the first person in Task 2, but there are other more academic ways of expressing an opinion. Try using *It* structures, e.g. *It is widely believed that* or *It is my opinion that...* You could also make use of adjectives which indirectly express your opinion, e.g. *There are many **persuasive** arguments about this.*

4b **Match statements a–c to paragraphs 1–3 below.**

1

Although older employees tend to be more senior and therefore earn higher salaries, it is arguable that they are more costly to retain. For one thing, their training costs tend to be negligible as they are highly experienced in their field. Then there's the argument that they are often willing to work part-time, which makes them a cheaper proposition. In addition, older employees benefit the economy because they are directly contributing to it. By contrast, if older workers are persuaded to retire, they will start to draw their pensions and therefore become a burden on the economy and on younger taxpayers.

2

Although younger workers' IT skills may be more up-to-date, it should be pointed out that older workers tend to be more adaptable than their younger counterparts. The older generation of workers has experienced a great more change in the workplace than young people and have had to adapt to the transformation of the workplace brought about by technology and global communication.

3

However, this does not really make economic sense. There are not a fixed number of jobs available in the economy and older and younger workers are not necessarily perfect substitutes for one another.

4c **Read the paragraphs again. Is this a balanced or a one-sided argument?**

4d **Read the advice and <u>underline</u> examples in the first paragraph which help the writer to argue against the opposing view.**

✏ EXAM TASK

5a **Work in pairs. Read the essay question and decide whether you broadly agree or disagree.**

> Some people think that men and women have different qualities. Therefore, specific jobs are better suited to men and others are more suitable for women.
>
> To what extent do you agree or disagree?

Give reasons for your answer and include any relevant examples from your knowledge or experience. Write at least 250 words.

5b **Plan and write your response to the exam task.**

Urbanisation and development

1 Work in pairs. Compare and contrast the two photographs of the same place. Why do you think these changes came about?

2a Divide the verbs in the box into five groups:

1 to make bigger **2** to take away **3** to add something new
4 to change into something else **5** to talk about change in general

> build   construct   convert   cut down   demolish   enlarge
> erect   expand   extend   industrialise   introduce   knock down
> make into   modernise   pull down   redevelop   remove   replace
> transform   turn into   urbanise

2b Describe a place in your town or city which has changed. Use the verbs in exercise 2a to help you. Which of these verbs can you make into nouns?

3a Work in pairs. Look at the map and discuss the questions.

a) How many periods of growth can you see? Which is the biggest and the smallest?

b) What do you think prompted and sustained the development?

c) Can you see any patterns in the development?

3b Read the sample answer and <u>underline</u> nine factual mistakes. Then correct them.

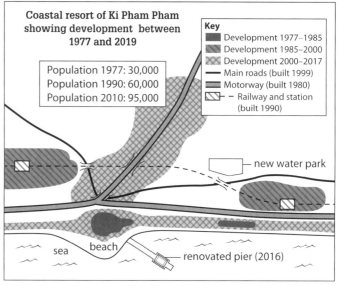

Coastal resort of Ki Pham Pham showing development between 1977 and 2019

Population 1977: 30,000
Population 1990: 60,000
Population 2010: 95,000

Key
■ Development 1977–1985
▨ Development 1985–2000
▧ Development 2000–2017
— Main roads (built 1999)
— Motorway (built 1980)
▭— Railway and station (built 1990)

— new water park
renovated pier (2016)
sea beach

The map shows the urbanisation of the seaside resort town of Ki Pham Pham over a period of over twenty years.

Initially, between 1977 and 1985, development was modest and concentrated near the coastline. However, between 1977 and 1990, there was a population explosion, with the number of residents going up more than threefold from 30,000 to 90,000. As a consequence, the residential areas decreased in size significantly. In addition, main roads and a railway were constructed to service the four new developments.

The first two decades of the 21st century saw even more development as the population continued to grow, increasing to 95,000 by 2020. New residential areas transformed the coastline as they were built along its stretch. Furthermore, a motorway was constructed to serve the area and as a result, more residential areas were built around it, to the north of the beachfront.

Further changes that took place were the modernisation of the waterpark on the beachfront and the renovation of the pier in 2015.

> **Exam tip**
>
> You will need to analyse the diagram or map carefully to see how and when changes took place. Pay close attention to any keys on the map or diagram.

3c Read the sample answer again and complete the statements with the words in the box.

> causes   chronological   end   main trends   paragraphs   periods   results

a) The writer describes the development in .... order.

b) The description identifies the main .... and .... of the phases of development.

c) The development is grouped into .... by the .... of development.

d) Miscellaneous developments, which don't fit with the ...., are placed at the .... of the answer.

4a The sample answer uses a number of ways of linking ideas together in a sentence. Match the ways a–f with examples 1–6 from the answer.

1 over a period of twenty years; in 2015, to the north of the beachfront

2 to help people to reach; to serve the area

3 with the number of residents in the area going up

4 as the population continued to grow; as they were built along its stretch

5 as a consequence; as a result

6 increasing to 95,000

a) a prepositional phrase and an -ing participle

b) an infinitive of purpose

c) a linking phrase of result (x2)

d) an -ing participle

e) as used as a conjunction to mean 'at the same time'

f) a prepositional phrase to indicate a location or time (x2)

4b Link the sentences using the ways described in exercise 4a.

1 The map illustrates the expansion of the town of Wotten-End. The period of development described is ten years.

2 The industrial area grew. At the same time, the shopping centre was built.

3 A bus route was constructed. The bus route helped children to get to school.

4 The residential area was built on the green 'belt' surrounding the city. A copse of trees had to be cut down.

5 The residential area increased in this period. It doubled in size.

6 The cinema was demolished. A new one was built. The new one was to the north of the old one.

7 In 1800, there was a housing crisis in the area. The number of residents decreased from 1 million to 500,000.

✏ EXAM TASK

5a Work in pairs. Look at the map below and decide how you will link and group the information.

5b The maps below show the village of Wotten-End in 1925 and 2015. Summarise the information by selecting and reporting the main features, and make comparisons where relevant. Write at least 150 words.

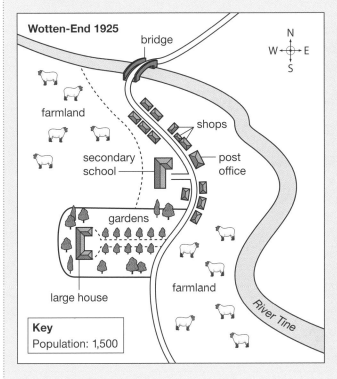

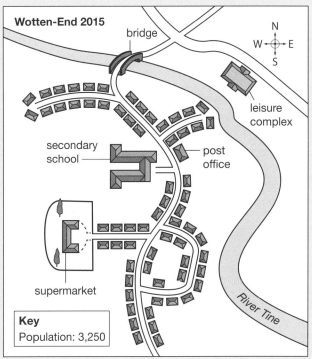

International travel

1 **Work in pairs. Discuss the questions.**

1 When was the last time you went abroad? Where did you go and why?

2 Do you think the cost of national and international travel has increased or decreased in recent years? Why do you think this is?

3 What are the advantages and disadvantages of a 'staycation' (holidaying at home) compared to going abroad on vacation?

2a **Read the essay title. Match it to a description of what the writer needs to do (A–C).**

> *Global travel has become cheaper in recent years and more countries are welcoming tourists. Do the advantages of this trend outweigh the disadvantages?*
>
> **a)** The writer needs to decide whether it's a good thing that international travel is cheaper.
>
> **b)** The writer needs to decide whether both cheap international travel and greater access to a variety of countries have more benefits than drawbacks.
>
> **c)** The writer needs to decide whether cheap international travel and access to more countries is beneficial.

2b **Work in small groups. Brainstorm the pros and cons of cheap international travel and greater access to a variety of countries. Discuss from the following perspectives: economic, environmental, cultural and safety.**

2c **Read the paragraphs from an sample essay below. Put them into a logical order.**

A .... Culturally speaking, encouraging tourists to visit countries that have been 'off the tourist trail' is a positive thing. A tourist is more likely to understand the cultures of a country if they experience them and is therefore likely to have a greater tolerance of difference.

B .... Finally, the encouragement of a greater variety of visitors is not without its health and safety risks. Tourists can inadvertently import and export diseases from a country. Unfortunately, they can also smuggle illegal objects and substances.

C ....From an individual traveller's point of view, reduced air travel costs can only be a good thing, economically speaking. It enables them to travel inexpensively. A greater volume of travellers is also financially beneficial to frequently flying budget airlines.

D .... However, frequent flights are not without environmental drawbacks; aeroplanes release more carbon dioxide per passenger than any other form of transport.

E .... In conclusion, I am not convinced that there are more benefits than drawbacks of cheaper travel and greater access to different countries. Although there are undoubtedly financial and cultural advantages, the environmental, cultural and health risks seem correspondingly high.

F .... International tourism is a growth industry, due both to the falling cost of airfares and to the increasing variety of countries that are opening their doors to visitors. There are many benefits to these developments, but there are also drawbacks. This essay will examine both from a number of perspectives.

G ....On the other hand, high volumes of tourists also have a potentially negative impact on a country's culture; historical sites can be damaged. What is more, tourists tend to have their own traditions which can be at odds with local customs.

Exam tip

When you are writing about advantages and disadvantages, you need to evaluate both parts of the statement. In Task 2, it's a good idea to plan your essay from different perspectives, or 'viewpoints'. This will help you to come up with a range of ideas.

2d **Read the paragraphs again. How does the writer introduce a particular perspective at the start of a paragraph? Complete the gaps in the sentences with phrases from exercise 2a.**

1 ...., visiting historical sites can increase our understanding of a country's traditions.

2 ...., international travel is a great deal more expensive than travelling in one's own country.

3 .... a tourist's ...., a holiday resort is a safe and convenient place to stay.

4 Flying is not .... environmental ....; anyone living under a flight path will attest to the noise pollution they have to endure.

5 High volumes of tourists have a .... on a country's coastal environment. It often necessitates the building of high rise hotels along coast lines.

3a **The writer uses linking words and phrases to help the reader to identify similar and contrasting ideas. Group the linking words that show similar additional ideas and those that show contrasting ideas.**

3b **Add the linkers in the box to your lists in exercise 3a.**

> besides   despite   even though   furthermore   in addition
> in contrast   nevertheless   nonetheless   though   yet

3c **Correct the mistakes in the sentences below.**

1 Despite to understand the environmental drawbacks of flying, tourists continue to travel abroad.

2 Although thousands of tourists visit The Taj Mahal annually, but the government does not attempt to restrict their numbers.

3 Tourists can import dangerous diseases into a country. In addition to, they can smuggle illegal items into a country.

4 People who don't travel often have preconceived ideas about other countries and cultures. Nevertheless, people who do travel often have a more realistic idea and don't make generalisations about other countries.

5 Tourists are often asked to cover their shoulders when visiting religious buildings. Even though, they often ignore this request.

6 Besides to release greenhouse gases, aeroplanes also create noise pollution.

7 Tourists often want to stay in remote places however they often complain when they find they can't get a wifi signal.

8 What is more, tourists should consider 'green holidays' in order to protect the environment. They should consider train travel as an alternative to flying.

✎ EXAM TASK

4a **Work in pairs. Plan a response to the essay title below.**

> Nowadays, scientists can travel to remote natural environments such as the South Pole. Tourists can also holiday in the middle of deserts and mountain ranges.
>
> What are the advantages and disadvantages of this development?

Give reasons for your answer and include any relevant examples from your own knowledge or experience. Write at least 250 words.

4b **Write your response to the essay question.**

Rocks on the move

1 Look at the photographs. What examples of weathering and erosion do they show? How do animals and humans contribute to erosion?

2a Look at the diagram of the rock cycle below. How many of the nouns in the shaded boxes can you change into verbs?

2b Complete the questions with verbs from exercise 2a.

1 What .... the eroded rocks down the mountain side into the sea?

2 What type of rock is .... onto the sea bed?

3 What happens to the rock after it has .... to form magma?

2c With a partner, look at the diagram and discuss the questions in exercise 2b.

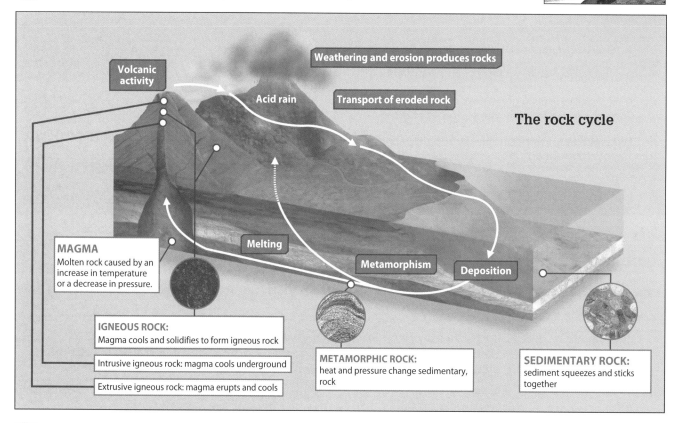

The rock cycle

Weathering and erosion produces rocks

Volcanic activity

Acid rain

Transport of eroded rock

Melting

Metamorphism

Deposition

MAGMA
Molten rock caused by an increase in temperature or a decrease in pressure.

IGNEOUS ROCK:
Magma cools and solidifies to form igneous rock

Intrusive igneous rock: magma cools underground

Extrusive igneous rock: magma erupts and cools

METAMORPHIC ROCK:
heat and pressure change sedimentary, rock

SEDIMENTARY ROCK:
sediment squeezes and sticks together

3a Read the tip box. Decide on a good point to start your description of the rock cycle.

3b Read the sentences about the rock cycle. Do they start from the same point in the cycle as you chose?

1a Rocks are weathered and eroded by animal activity, acid rain and dramatic changes in temperature.

1b Animal activity, acid rain and dramatic changes in temperature cause rocks to weather and erode.

3c Which sentence in exercise 3b emphasises that rocks are the focus of the description?

Exam tip

When describing a natural cycle, it is not always obvious where you should start the description. Look for a main cause of an important part of the cycle. For example, in the water cycle, the sun causes the water to evaporate, which begins the cycle.

4a Read the tip box. Three of the sentences work better in the passive voice. Rewrite them so that the rock is the focus of the description.

1 Rivers transport the eroded rocks down mountain sides and deposit them into the ocean.

2 The weight of the water and other materials squeezes and cements the eroded rock together.

3 Heat and pressure change sedimentary rock into metamorphic rock.

4 Metamorphic rock either gradually works its way up to the earth's surface, or it melts to form magma.

5 The magma then cools underground or erupts and cools on the Earth's surface.

4b Extra marks are awarded in IELTS if additional information from the diagram is added to the description to explain the process in more detail. Work in pairs. Discuss where you could add the details below to the sentences in exercise 4a.

1 via volcanic activity

2 where the elements and other forces begin the weathering process.

3 where they sink to the bottom as sediment.

4 in order to form sedimentary rock.

4c In your pairs, decide which of the linking words in the box could be used in the description and details in exercises 4a and 4b.

> at other times   at times   eventually   finally   once again

✏ EXAM TASK

5a Plan your description of the nitrogen cycle illustrated below. You should spend about 20 minutes on this task.

The diagram below shows the movement of nitrogen in its different forms around the natural environment. Summarise the information by selecting and reporting the main features, and make comparisons where relevant. Write at least 150 words.

5b Write your description of the cycle. Write at least 150 words.

Doing damage

1a **Match the phrases to the environmental problems in the photographs.**

waste

air pollution

urban overpopulation

a) bring about a water shortage

b) cause an increase in bacteria, spread of malaria-carrying mosquitoes

c) cause an increase in forest fires and drought

d) cause damage to ecosystems

e) cause icebergs to melt

f) cause respiratory-related health problems

g) damage animals' habitats, causing extinction

h) encourage people to over-exploit natural resources

i) encourage pests to spread

j) give off harmful gases

k) lead to an elevated crime rate

l) leak toxic chemicals into our water supply

m) make water levels rise and floods occur

n) cause a rise in the earth's temperature

o) trap sea and land animals

1b **Work in pairs. Discuss which of the problems in the pictures in exercise 1a does the most damage to our environment. Give reasons for your answers.**

2a **Read the exam task. Discuss the questions below.**

Describe some ways in which mankind is harming the environment. What can governments do to address these problems? What can individuals do?

1 Do you need to describe all types of environmental damage? How many do you think you could realistically describe in an essay of approximately 250 words?

2 How many paragraphs do you think you need to answer the essay (including the introduction and conclusion)? What would the main subject of each paragraph be?

3 Does your essay need to dedicate more space to problems or solutions, do you think?

> **Exam tip**
>
> Sometimes the wording of IELTS Writing tasks is very general, for e.g. 'Describe some environmental problems.' Choose the problems that you know the most about and describe only these. Otherwise, you will write too much and risk running out of time.

2b **Read the sample essay. How has the writer addressed the issues in 1-3 in exercise 2a?**

Humans are responsible for causing a great deal of damage to the environment. However, there are steps that we can take in order to tackle the problems we've caused and to decrease the harm done. This essay will outline two of the main environmental problems and suggest measures that both the government and individuals can take to address these issues.

An increase in air pollution and waste are two of the most serious threats to our environment. Emissions of harmful gases from industrial plants and vehicles lead to global warming, which in turn result in a greater incidence of floods and drought, as well as a more rapid spread of diseases. On the other hand, the growth in food waste and plastic packaging causes landfill sites to expand and to pollute nearby areas with their toxic runoff. As plastic doesn't decompose, it becomes stuck in ecosystems, strangling animals and ruining areas of natural beauty.

Governments could reduce air pollution. For instance, they could introduce legislation in order to limit emissions and impose higher taxes for environmentally unfriendly vehicles. At the same time, they could improve the public transport infrastructure. If driving became too expensive and people had a viable alternative, they would opt for public transport.

Individuals also need to take responsibility for the affect they are having on the environment. They should avoid buying food stuffs which have a lot of packaging and should recycle. As well as using reusable bags, they could also make an effort to create meals from leftovers, rather than throwing food away.

In conclusion, both national governments and individuals must play their part in solving environmental issues such as global warming and waste. If we don't, it is likely that before very soon, our world will not be inhabitable.

3 Select the right verb to go with each noun phrase. You can re-use verbs.

> **1** play **2** make **3** have **4** impose **5** improve
> **6** avoid **7** tackle **8** decrease **9** take **10** address

Noun	
a) a viable alternative	**h)** measures
b) buying foodstuffs	**i)** part
c) effort	**j)** problems
d) harm	**k)** responsibility
e) higher taxes	**l)** reusable bags
f) infrastructure	**m)** steps
g) issues	

4a Look at paragraph 2 of the essay in exercise 2b. Underline the verb + noun collocations.

4b Underline two conditional structures in the sample essay. Which structure:

a) describes a situation that is likely to happen in the future?

b) describes the possible consequence of a hypothetical option, which is not yet a reality?

c) includes the present tense in the conditional clause and 'will' in the main clause?

d) includes the past tense in the conditional clause and 'would' in the main clause?

5 Complete the sentence beginnings with your own ideas.

1 If the population continues to expand at the same rate …

2 If we forced supermarkets to give away produce that it didn't sell …

3 If the government banned deforestation …

4 If governments forced companies to use only renewable energy …

5 If polar icecaps continue to melt ….

6 If we don't improve our flood defences …

7 If the whole world switched to used nuclear energy only …

8 If governments introduced a tax on landfill sites …

✎ EXAM TASK

6a Read the Writing Task 2 question. Do you need to describe problems as well as solutions?

> With rapidly growing populations and cities, many countries are losing their natural beauty spots. What benefits are there to preserving beauty spots? How can this issue be solved?

Exam tip

Use conditional sentences to make predictions and hypotheses about the consequences of a particular problem or solution in an essay.

6b Write your essay. Write at least 250 words.

60 mins

All the right gear

1a Work in pairs. List the clothing and equipment you need to practise the sports in the box.

> aerobics basketball football golf skateboarding tennis

1b What are the most important characteristics of running shoes or trainers? Rank the characteristics in the box from most to least important. Give reasons for your answers.

> absorbent breathable comfortable cushioned durable fashionable

2a Look at the diagram of the running shoe manufacturing process. Answer the questions.

  1 Which verbs would you use to describe each stage?

  2 What do you think the point is of each part of the process?

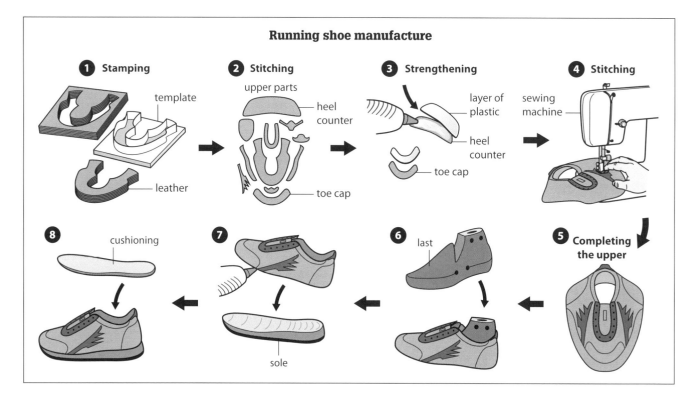

2b Read the sample process description. Which linking words are used to describe the reason behind specific stages?

The diagram illustrates the processes involved in the manufacture of a running shoe, from the cutting of the 'upper' to the gluing on of the sole.

First of all, the pieces of leather comprising the top parts of the shoe are cut out of leather, using a template. Next, the pieces of leather known as the toe cap and heel counter are reinforced with plastic so that they can make the toe and the heel of the running shoe more durable. After that, all of the upper parts of the trainer are assembled and sewn together in order to form the upper. The upper is then moulded around a 'last' so that it forms the desired shape of the trainer.

Once the upper is ready, glue is applied to the sole of the trainer and the upper and sole are joined together. Finally, synthetic cushioning is inserted into the running shoe so as to reduce the impact when a runner puts his or her foot on the floor at speed.

> **Exam tip**
>
> You can describe the reasons behind stages of the process using linkers such as *so as to, so that, in order to.*

PHOTOCOPIABLE

2c The diagram will not give you all of the verbs that you need to describe the process, so it's important to learn the different forms of as many verbs as you can. Match the verbs in the sample description to the definitions.

1 to stick two things together using a thick liquid ....

2 to make something stronger by adding another layer ....

3 to group different parts together in a logical order or arrangement ....

4 to attach parts with a needle and thread ....

5 to change the shape of a material by forming it around a hard surface ....

6 to put something inside another thing ....

7 to make something less, to decrease ....

2d Without looking back at the description, use present and passive participles to join each of these sentences together. Then, compare the process description to your answers.

1 First of all, pieces of leather are cut out of a large piece of leather. The pieces of leather comprise the top part of the shoe.

2 Next, the pieces of leather around the toe and heel of the trainer are reinforced with plastic. The pieces of leather are known as the toe cap and heel counter.

> **Exam tip**
>
> Vary your use of relative clauses and the passive by using present and past participles in your process description.

✏ EXAM TASK

3a Work in pairs. Look at the diagram of some stages in the manufacture of a skateboard. Which verbs do you need to describe it?

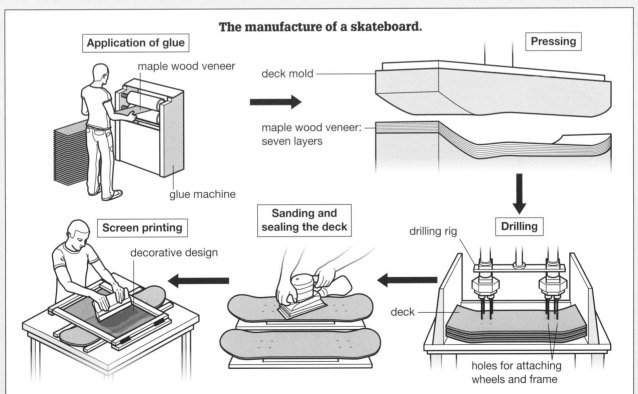

The manufacture of a skateboard.

3b Summarise the information in the diagram by selecting and reporting the main features and make comparisons where relevant. Write at least 150 words.

60 mins

The dangers of technology

1a Work in pairs. How many social media sites can you name? How many do you have installed on your phone or tablet? What does each one allow you to do?

1b in your pairs, discuss the meaning of the internet safety issues a–c. Use the words in the wordcloud to help you.

a) cyberbullying   b) inappropriate content   c) identity theft

1c Imagine that you are the parent of a teenager who is experiencing one of the issues in exercise 1b. Discuss how you would help your son or daughter to solve their problem.

Hacked internet accounts
Vulnerable to new influences
embarrassing photos uploaded
Unwittingly reveal personal details
Being secretive   **Swearing**
Gambling sites   devastating
Fake profiles   **Saying offensive things**
Abusive trolling **Images of violence or cruelty**
Difficult to monitor Sites that encourage vandalism
Adopt extreme views
Unexpected bills   Incessant
Unmoderated chatrooms   **Anonymity**
Threatening or malicious text messages
Need for identity and belonging
Mistrust of mainstream media
terrorism or eating disorders
crime

2a Read the essay task and decide how to approach it. Answer the questions.

a) which problems you will focus on

b) which solutions you will suggest

c) how you will paraphrase the key words underlined in the essay task

> The development of social media means that an increasing number of young people have unsupervised access to the internet in order to meet and chat with friends. Describe some problems this creates and solutions to deal with these problems.

2b Read the sample essay. Decide the type of information a–d that is missing from the gaps.

a) a consequence of a problem   c) an example of a problem

b) a solution   d) an introduction of a problem

The growth in the range of social media sites available makes it possible for teenagers to use them to socialise online without being monitored. This makes young people vulnerable to online threats. This essay will explore these potential dangers and suggest some steps that adults can take to try to protect children. Cyberbullying is one of the most wide-spread problems on social media.

1 .... Cyberbullying is perhaps more damaging than the face-to-face equivalent because the bully can remain anonymous and can reach the victim wherever they are. **2** .... Young people can unwittingly reveal a lot of personal details, such as their name, address and birthday online. **3** .... This can lead to hackers using the innocent teenager's details in order to commit a crime.

There are, however, steps that adults can take to safeguard their children. It may be tempting for parents to restrict a child's internet use or even confiscate their devices. In my experience though, this may lead to the child becoming secretive. **4** .... talking to them about what they get up to online. It is also vital to educate young people about internet safety, so thatthey can tackle the issues they face.

To sum up, although the threats that social media poses towards young people are severe and very real, it is possible to avoid teenagers suffering by establishing trusting, communicative relationships and by educating young people so that they can help themselves.

2c **Complete items 1-4 in the sample essay with the sentences (a-d).**

a) Another issue facing young social media users is identity theft.

b) Instead, it is better to build a trusting relationship with a teenager from a young age

c) Teenagers can be sent malicious text messages, be banned from groups by their peers and have embarrassing photos uploaded.

d) They can suffer psychological, physical and financial damage.

2d **Complete the table with the correct form of the academic words from the sample essay.**

noun	verb	adjective
commitment	1	committed
psychology / psychologist	–	2 ....
finance	finance	3 ....
restriction	4	restrictive
establishment	5	established
summary	6 .... / summarise	–
communication	communicate	7 ....

✏ EXAM TASK

3a **Read the exam task. Plan your response, using the planning outline below to help you.**

These days, many children have access to computers and a large number play computer games. What negative effects does playing computer games have on children and what can be done to reduce these effects?

Introduction	Paraphrase of key words in essay title
First paragraph	Problem
	Explanation / examples
	Consequence
	Problem
	Explanation / example
Second paragraph	Consequence of problem
	Solutions
	Explanation / example of solutions
	Solution
	Explanation / example of solutions
Conclusion	Summing up of arguments

3b **Write your essay. Write at least 250 words.**

Going green

1 Work in pairs. Think of a film that you've enjoyed which features special effects. Describe them to your partner.

2 Do you think the scene in the photograph was filmed 'on location' or created in a different way?

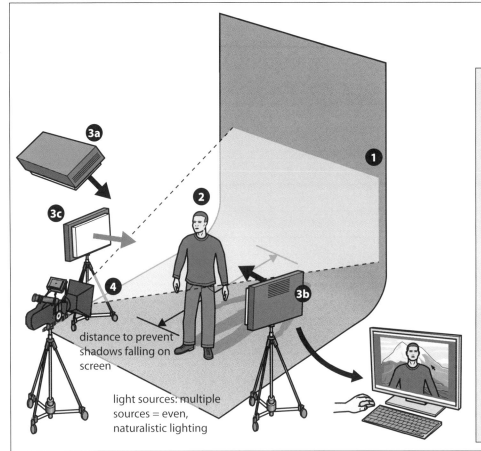

Key

1 green screen background: green made transparent after filming to allow different backgrounds behind actor(keying)

2 actor / talent: must not wear green or reflective clothing / accessories

3 light sources: multiple sources = even, naturalistic lighting.

  3a backlight, overhead, separates actor from background

  3b keylight: lights the actor's face and body, must be diffused light

  3c fill light: lights the other side of the actor's face and body

4 camera view

distance to prevent shadows falling on screen

light sources: multiple sources = even, naturalistic lighting

3 Look at the diagram of a 'green screen' filming set-up which is used to achieve special effects in film and television. Using the diagram to help you, complete the sample diagram description.

The diagram shows a 'green screen' filming set up, which is a system that enables actors to be superimposed on any background so as to achieve the special effects seen in films. The set-up consists of the green screen background, the **1** .... or 'talent', a number of **2** .... and cameras. The colour of the screen is significant; green facilitates being made translucent or invisible when the actor is superimposed onto a different background.

There are a variety of different light sources, which allow the lighting to look as **3** .... as possible. The **4** .... is positioned overhead in order to separate the actor from the background. The keylight is located to one side of the actor and this lights the actor's face and body. The **5** ...., positioned at the other side of the actor, lights the other side of their face. As we can see from the diagram, the talent stands at a specified distance from the green screen in order to prevent the light that hits them casting a **6** .... on the screen behind them.

4a Complete the table with useful language for Task 1 of a diagram description. Then check your answers in the sample description.

It's a device / **1** .... / tool / machine which / that	**2** .... **3** .... prevents .... **4** .... / in order that+ noun / in order to+ verb / so that + noun / **5** .... + verb
It **6** .... It comprises of ... It's made up of a ... It's divided into ...	which is / are used for ...
There's a ... which	enable(s) ... to ... allow(s) the ... of ... **7** .... (from) +ing

4b Choose two of the objects in the box. Write a short description of each object using the language from exercise 4a.

> air conditioning unit   burglar alarm   cashpoint   photocopier   vacuum cleaner   washing machine

4c In pairs, take turns to read your descriptions of the objects. Ask your partner to guess the name of the object.

Exam tip

When describing an object, it's often better to start with an object's appearance and key parts before going on to talk about its function in detail.

✏ EXAM TASK

5a Number the parts of the diagram description in the order in which you would write about them.

.... Key parts involved in the piano's action   .... Stages of action

.... Summary of what the diagram shows

5b Plan and write your description.

The diagram below shows a cross-section of a piano and its working parts. Summarise the information in the diagram by selecting and reporting the main features and making comparisons where relevant. Write at least 150 words.

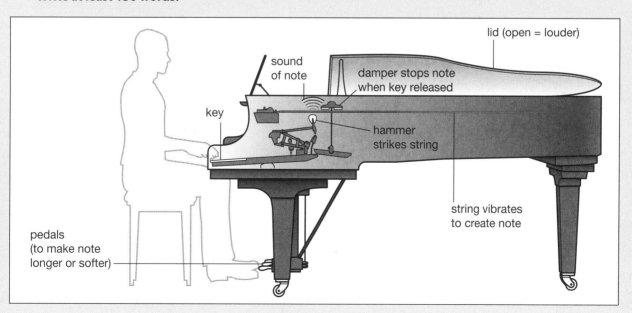

lid (open = louder)

sound of note

damper stops note when key released

key

hammer strikes string

string vibrates to create note

pedals (to make note longer or softer)

Artistic licence

1a **Work in pairs. Look at the picture and discuss the questions.**

1 Have you ever taken a 'selfie' in front of a work of art?

2 Do you remember the work of art?

3 What did you do with the selfie after your gallery visit?

4 What is the impact of taking selfies in a gallery?

1b **Choose the option that is true for you. Then compare your answer with your partner.**

If I wanted to find out more about a work of art, I would:

a look it up online   **b** research it in a book

c visit it in an art gallery   **d** a combination of a–c

2 **Read the exam question. Which of these things are you NOT required to do?**

A Explain the cause of a change

B Explain the effects of a change

C Give your opinion of a change

> Thanks to developments in technology, we can now view art in many different ways. In what ways has this changed the public's relationship with art and with art galleries? Has this been a positive or negative development?

Exam tip

With cause and effect essays, you are not always asked to explain or describe the cause of a development. Sometimes the question asks you to concentrate on the effects or asks for your opinion. Make sure you read the question carefully.

3a **Read the sample essay, ignoring the bolding and the gaps. Does the writer think that technology has had a positive or negative development on the public's relationship with art?**

A Technology has undoubtedly altered our experience of art. It is now possible to look up almost any image online or to learn about an artwork through an audio and video device on a gallery visit. This essay will explore and evaluate the impact of our viewing art on a screen.

B **1 It** is now commonplace to look at art online. Some people will follow **2 this** up with a visit to the art gallery in order to view the 'real thing'. Others, however, feel that the virtual experience will suffice. **3 This** inevitably results in fewer visits to art galleries, **4 which** decreases the income of art institutions. Arguably, the virtual existence of an artwork also makes **5 it** more commonplace. **6 This** could lead to people ceasing to appreciate **7 its** details and value.

C Galleries have tried to keep up with the popularity of technology by including information about **8 their** collections on their websites and by giving visitors the opportunity to have the virtual experience of an artwork alongside the real **9 one**. Reading research **10** .... has been written about an artwork before seeing **11** .... 'in the flesh' can heighten people's appreciation of **12** .... However, the expert's opinion often replaces a viewer's interpretation, and **13** .... can prevent original analysis. What is more, reading about a work of art while standing in front of **14** .... can be distracting.

D In conclusion, although technology increases the accessibility of art and sometimes results in our learning more about a work of art, **15** .... can also decrease art's value in the viewer's eyes and prevent us from interpreting **16** .... in our own personal way. On balance, I feel that technology has a negative impact on our experience of art.

3b Look at the numbered words in bold 1–9 in the sample essay. Complete the table with the correct information.

Word	Type of information it refers to	Example from essay
it	a 'dummy' pronoun used when the sentence does not have a subject. often used with phrases such as it is a fact that… / it is widely believed that …	
it	refers backwards or forwards to a noun phrase or an idea	
its	the possessive of a pronoun	
this	refers backwards or forwards to a phrase or idea	
which	a relative pronoun which replaces the object of the previous clause	
one	refers backwards or forwards to a singular noun	
their	the possessive plural pronoun	

3c Complete the numbered gaps in bold 10–16 with the correct word. All the words you need are in the table in exercise 3b.

Exam tip

Using words such as pronouns instead of repeating words and ideas in your essay is a good way of increasing the cohesion of your essay. Allow enough time for checking and correcting the cohesion of your essay.

✎ EXAM TASK

4a Read the exam task and the paragraph below it. Which words could you delete and replace to make the paragraph more cohesive?

Nowadays, it is possible to download copyrighted music and books from the internet at a low cost or at no charge at all. In what ways has this affected the musicians and authors? Has this been a positive or negative development?

…On the other hand, illegal downloads can have a positive effect on the artist. The artist can find new and innovative ways of selling the artist's music. For example, it is possible to release a digital album for free as well as an album at a higher price. This album would have exclusive content and personal details. Fans would be prepared to pay for this exclusive content. New bands can also offer a single from a new album to download. Making the single available often encourages fans to buy the whole album and to spread the word about the album on social media. Spreading the word about the album increases the album's likelihood of selling well when the album is released.

4b Plan and write an essay in response to the exam task. Write at least 250 words.

60 mins

Mechanical motion

1a Number the modes of transport in the order that you think they were invented.

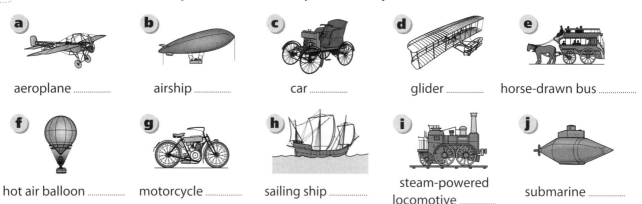

a aeroplane ....

b airship ....

c car ....

d glider ....

e horse-drawn bus ....

f hot air balloon ....

g motorcycle ....

h sailing ship ....

i steam-powered locomotive ....

j submarine ....

1b Work in pairs. Choose four modes of transport from exercise 1a. Identify similarities and differences between them. Think about:

shape   function   size

2a Look at the diagrams, which show stages in the development of the bicycle. Name the different parts of each of the bicycles. Use the topic vocabulary in the box to help you.

> chain   frame   gear   handlebar   mudguard
> pedal   saddle   wheel

Exam tip

Diagrams always have some labels, but sometimes don't include the key words which identify the main parts of an object. It is a good idea to learn how to describe the parts of everyday objects.

2b Which overall trend does NOT describe the bicycle's general development?

A It became smaller

B It became easier to pedal

C It became more comfortable

D It became lighter

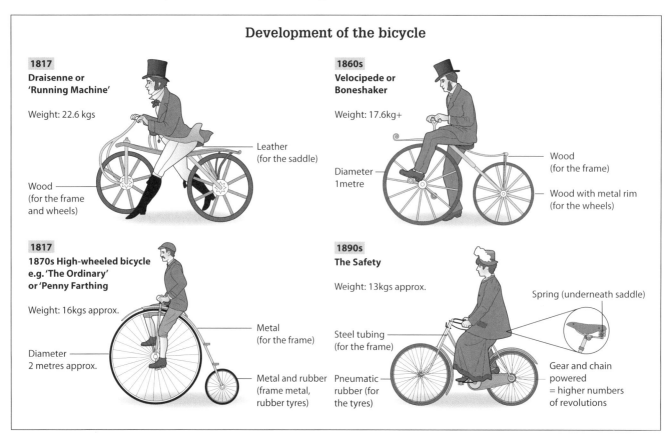

Development of the bicycle

1817
Draisenne or 'Running Machine'
Weight: 22.6 kgs
Wood (for the frame and wheels)
Leather (for the saddle)

1860s
Velocipede or Boneshaker
Weight: 17.6kg+
Diameter 1metre
Wood (for the frame)
Wood with metal rim (for the wheels)

1817
1870s High-wheeled bicycle e.g. 'The Ordinary' or 'Penny Farthing
Weight: 16kgs approx.
Diameter 2 metres approx.
Metal (for the frame)
Metal and rubber (frame metal, rubber tyres)

1890s
The Safety
Weight: 13kgs approx.
Steel tubing (for the frame)
Pneumatic rubber (for the tyres)
Spring (underneath saddle)
Gear and chain powered = higher numbers of revolutions

3a   **Read the sample description of the bicycle's evolution. <u>Underline</u> words which have a similar meaning to:**

1 become available   **2** moved   **3** the bicycle that came before

The diagrams illustrate the progression of the bicycle's design in the 19th century. All of the bicycles consist of a frame and two wheels. The Draisenne, invented in 1817, weighed over 22 kilograms and had a wooden frame and wheels. It was powered by the rider's feet only. Then the velocipede or 'boneshaker' appeared. It had larger wheels than the Draisenne; they were around 1 metre in diameter, and the whole bicycle was lighter. The velocipede had pedals, although it didn't have a chain or gears, meaning the wheel revolutions were quite low.

Different types of high-wheeled bicycles, for example, the Penny Farthing, were introduced a decade later. These bicycles were far taller than earlier models because their front wheels had a larger diameter, which meant that they could be propelled considerably further. Finally, in the late 1890s, the Safety bicycle became popular. Its pneumatic rubber wheels meant that it was much more comfortable and its steel tubing frame meant it was also lighter. It was also powered by a chain and gears, enabling the rider to move forward more easily and quickly.

Overall, the development of the bicycle has been one of decreasing weight and increasing comfort and speed.

3b   **<u>Underline</u> comparative structures in the sample description. Which adverbs modify adjectives and comparative adjectives in the description? Do they emphasise or weaken the word that follows them?**

3c   **<u>Find</u> useful language, describing structure, size / weight and shape, in the example description in sample 3a.**

> **Exam tip**
>
> Don't repeat the word 'invented' when you describe the development of an object. Using synonyms shows that you have a wide-ranging vocabulary.

✏ EXAM TASK

4   **Plan and write a response to the exam task.**

The diagram below shows the development of the bus. Summarise the information in the diagram by selecting and reporting the main features and making comparisons where relevant. Write at least 150 words.

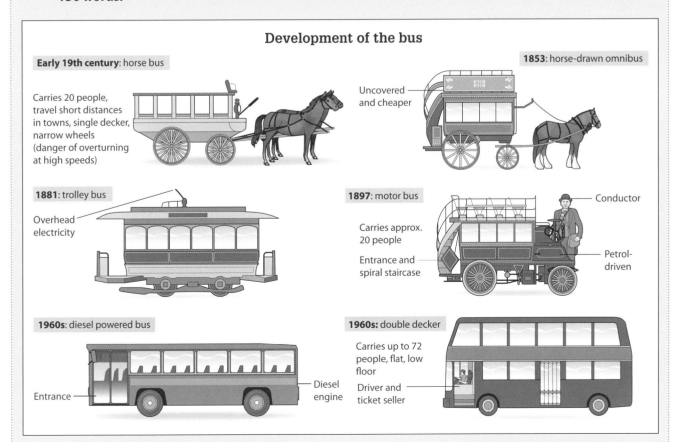

Development of the bus

Early 19th century: horse bus — Carries 20 people, travel short distances in towns, single decker, narrow wheels (danger of overturning at high speeds)

1853: horse-drawn omnibus — Uncovered and cheaper

1881: trolley bus — Overhead electricity

1897: motor bus — Carries approx. 20 people, Entrance and spiral staircase, Conductor, Petrol-driven

1960s: diesel powered bus — Entrance, Diesel engine

1960s: double decker — Carries up to 72 people, flat, low floor, Driver and ticket seller

60 mins

Global gridlock

1a **Read the quote from Bill Ford, executive chairman of Ford Motor Co.**

> "We're going to clean up cars, and I love that we're doing it, but a clean traffic jam is still a traffic jam."

1b **Work in pairs. Look at the photos which describe four possible solutions to the problem described in exercise 1a. Discuss the advantages and disadvantages of each.**

Driverless electric vehicles that communicate with one another in Abu Dhab

New York's dedicated traffic only and pedestrian only zones

London's public cycle scheme

Octopus card can be used for most public transport in Hong Kong

2a **Read the three essay questions. Match each to essay types 1–3.**

1 an opinion essay ....

2 a cause and effect essay .... '

3 a problem solution essay ....

A Persuading commuters to use public transport is the best way to solve traffic problems in cities. To what extent do you agree or disagree?

B Traffic jams are becoming a significant problem for many major cities. Suggest some steps that could be taken to reduce traffic in big cities.

C In cities and towns all over the world the high volume of traffic is a problem. What are the causes of this and what impact does it have on people living in the cities and towns?

2b **Read part of an essay plan. Which essay question in exercise 2a does it answer?**

For	Against
● More environmentally friendly: Buses and trains accommodate more people than cars: less traffic on the road and less pollution. ● Government would be forced to improve 'tired' public transport systems ● If public transport were free, everyone would use it. ● It would create jobs.	● Impractical: sometimes the bus routes don't go where people need to get to, or at the right time. Often existing bus services are poor – puts more strain on them. ● Expensive for governments and individuals: new public transport systems would be needed. Tickets for buses and trains aren't cheap ● Bad economically: damage car sales ● Unfeasible: some people will never be persuaded to use public transport. ● Un-environmentally friendly: buses are not eco-friendly. More on the roads mean more pollution.

2c **Read the essay plan again. Overall, do you think the writer agrees or disagrees with the statement in essay question A?**

2d **Read a sample conclusion to essay question A and a teacher's comments. Discuss what the criteria are for writing an effective conclusion.**

It is undeniable that there are many arguments in favour of an increased use of public transport. A greater number of buses and a higher frequency of trains would result in fewer cars on the roads and therefore less pollution. However, what is needed is a practical, feasible solution to the traffic congestion problem. Unfortunately, many existing public transport systems offer a poor service and the vehicles are old and not environmentally friendly. Only by replacing them with a completely new system would the environment benefit substantially and this would be economically unfeasible, especially during our current financial crisis. It would also take an impractically long time to overhaul public transport systems. On balance, then, I believe that encouraging commuters to use public transport rather than cars is not the best solution. Instead, it is a better idea to reduce traffic on the roads by introducing a congestion charge.

An excellent rephrasing of the main question you're answering

[It is undeniable that there are many arguments in favour of an increased use of public transport.] A greater number of buses and a higher frequency of trains would result in fewer cars on the roads and therefore less pollution. However, what is needed is a practical, feasible solution to the traffic congestion problem.

Good summarising of main points in essay

Unfortunately, many existing public transport systems offer a poor service and the vehicles are old and not environmentally friendly. Only by replacing them with a completely new system would the environment benefit substantially and this would be economically unfeasible, especially during our current financial crisis. It would also take an impractically long time to overhaul public transport systems.] On balance, then, I believe that encouraging commuters to use public transport rather than cars is not the best solution.] Instead, it is a better idea, to reduce traffic on the roads by introducing a congestion charge.]

Good summarising of main points in essay

This is the first time you've mentioned the solution. also, do you need to suggest other solutions?

3 **Read the sample essay conclusion in exercise 2d again. Underline structures which make the sentence more emphatic.**

Exam tip

Your conclusion will depend on the type of essay question you answer. If it is an opinion essay, you need to summarise your stance, but if it's a problem-solution essay, you need to summarise the solutions included in the main body. In all types of essay, however, try not to include new ideas in your conclusion.

✐ EXAM TASK

4a **Plan an essay to answer the below exam task.**

Increasing the price of petrol is the best way to solve growing traffic and pollution problems. To what extent do you agree or disagree? What other measures do you think might be effective?

Give reasons for your answer and include any relevant examples from your own knowledge or experience. Write at least 250 words.

4b **Write the conclusion to your planned essay, using the criteria in exercise 2d and emphatic structures where possible.**

60 mins

Sweet tooth

1 Work in pairs. Look at the fruit juice food label. How many teaspoons of sugar does it contain?
(1 teaspoon = 5 g)

- Do you and your partner like sugary foods? Which of you eats the most sugar per day? How do you feel after you've eaten a lot of sugar?
- How can we become more aware of the sugar content of foods? How can we cut back on sugar?

Nutrition facts

Serving Sizes: 8 fl oz (240ml)

Amount per serving	
Calories 120 g	Calories from fat 0

	% Daily value*
Total fat 0 g	0%
Saturated fat 0 g	0%
Trans fat 0 g	
Cholesterol 0 g	0%
Sodium 10 mg	0%
Potassium 200 mg	6%
Total Carbohydrate 31 g	10%
Dietary fibre 2 g	8%
Sugars 25 g	

UK sugar intake compared to the recommended maximum of 5% energy

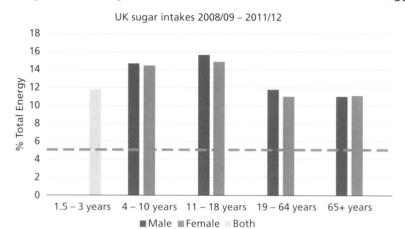

UK sugar intakes 2008/09 – 2011/12

■Male ■Female ▨Both

Contributors to sugar intake in the UK –
children aged 4 to 18 years

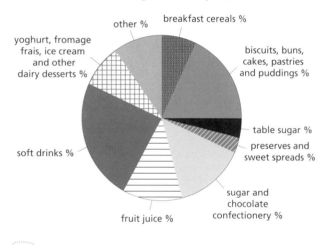

Contributors to sugar intake in the UK –
adults aged 19 to 64 years

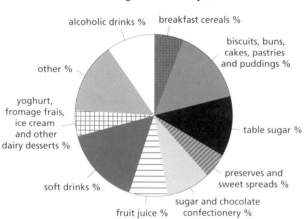

2a Look at the graph and charts. How do they relate to one another? Tick the correct options.

1 They show the same age groups. ☐

2 They contain data from the same time period. ☐

3 Both the graph and charts break down sugar intake by gender. ☐

4 The graph look at sugar intake as a total and the pie charts break it down by food type. ☐

2b Read the first paragraph of the graph and chart description.
Check your answers to exercise 2a.

The bar graph illustrates the amount of sugar people between the ages of one and a half and 65 years of age consumed over four years as a percentage of their total energy intake, in comparison to the recommended maximum energy percentage. The two pie charts break the sugar consumption of three of the age groups included in the graph into different food groups.

Exam tip

When you are comparing data in two or three charts, show in your opening paragraph how one set of data relates to another.

2c Underline the words in the first paragraph which are different to the words in the title of the graphs.

2d Work in pairs. Discuss the questions.

1 What are the most significant pieces of information in:

A the graph   **B** the pie charts

2 Which information does not need to be mentioned?

3 Which do you think you would start your description with: the data in the graph or the pie charts? Give reasons for your answer.

3a Read the body of a sample graph description and compare it to your answers to exercise 2d.

Looking at the graph first, we can see that both males and females of 11–18 years took in the highest amounts of sugar, at 16 and 15.2 percent of their food energy **respectively**. Males and females in the 4–10 years age group consumed nearly <u>as much sugar</u>, at 14.8 and 14.6 percent. The age group which consumed the lowest amount of sugar were the 65 years olds and up.

It is clear when comparing the graph to the pie charts that 4 to 18 year olds who ate the most sugar **did so** in the form of soft drinks, and biscuits, cakes and puddings; these two food groups contributed 45 and 30 percent. In contrast adults of 19 to 64 years consumed <u>far more</u> table sugar, at 17% as opposed to around 7% in the younger age groups. This suggests that people of ages 65 upwards, who consume the least sugar, avoid foods which are inherently high in sugar and prefer to add sugar to food.

3b In Task 1, when you have a limited number of words, it's important to avoid repetition.

1 Look at the words in **bold** in the sample description. How do they help the writer to avoid repetition?

2 Look at the <u>underlined</u> words in the sample description. Which part of the comparative structure is not included?

✏ EXAM TASK

4 Plan and write a description of the following table and graph. Summarise the information in the table and graph by selecting and reporting the main features and making comparisons where relevant. Write at least 150 words.

Teen exposure to TV advertising by product type and age group

| | Teens (12-17 years) | | |
Product type	Average # of ads viewed	% total ads viewed	Teen: adult targeted ratio
Lunch/dinner items	832.0	59%	0.86
Value menu/combo meals	175.0	12%	0.82
Kids' meals	119.6	8%	2.86
Snacks/desserts	87.9	6%	0.88
Breakfast items	53.6	4%	0.88
Promotion only	39.5	3%	1.09
Branding only	39.2	3%	0.93
Healthy options	35.4	3%	0.83
Coffee beverages	31.5	2%	0.86

Highlighting indicates higher-than-expected teen:adult targeted ratios
Source: Nielsen (2012) National TV only

Trends in exposure to TV advertising for all fast food restaurants by age group

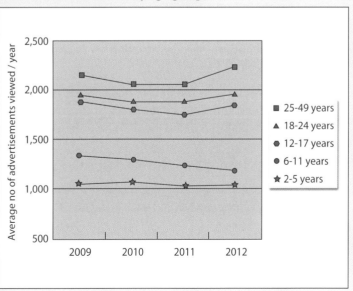

Average no of advertisements viewed / year

■ 25-49 years
▲ 18-24 years
● 12-17 years
● 6-11 years
★ 2-5 years

Modern maladies

1 **Look at the infographic and information on diabetes. What do you learn about a) diabetes and its causes? b) our lifestyle choices?**

Type 2 diabetes

Type 2 diabetes (formerly called non-insulin-dependent or adult-onset) results from the body's ineffective use of insulin. Type 2 diabetes comprises the majority of people with diabetes around the world, and is largely the result of excess body weight and physical inactivity.

Until recently, this type of diabetes was seen only in adults but it is now also occurring increasingly frequently in children.

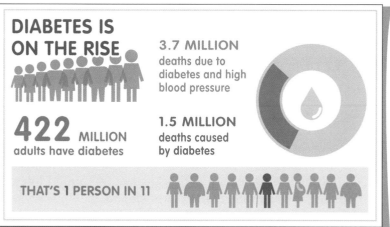

2a **Read the sample essay questions below. How could you use diabetes as an example to respond to each of them?**

1 Research indicates that our genetic makeup has far more influence on our weight than our diet or exercise regime. Which do you consider to be the major influence?

2 Recent research shows that our diets have changed because of our lifestyles. In what ways have our lifestyles affected our diets? Has this become a positive or negative development?

3 Some people believe that it is the responsibility of individuals to take care of their own health and diet rather than to rely on public health services. To what extent do you agree or disagree?

2b **Which of the questions requires the candidate to:**

1 respond to two questions in their essay?

2 choose one factor?

3 discuss one view and give your opinion?

3 **Read two sample introductions to essay question 2 in exercise 2a. Which do you think is most successful? Give reasons for your answer.**

1 It has been found that the way we live nowadays has brought about changes to the food and drink we choose to consume. It is my view that these changes have had an overwhelmingly negative impact on our diet and health.

2 The way we currently live has, without doubt, altered our diets in a number of ways, such as encouraging us to eat more convenience food and to consume increasing quantities of energy-boosting drinks. It is my view that overall, our diet is much more unhealthy as a result of our lifestyle.

4a **Work in pairs. Discuss how you would structure your response to question 2 in exercise 2a. Answer the questions.**

1 How many paragraphs would your essay need?

2 What would be the main subject of each paragraph?

3 Would one paragraph be more objective and the other be more subjective? Why / why not?

Exam tip

In double question IELTS essays, you need to make sure that you identify both parts of the question in your introduction and make your opinion clear.

4b Work in pairs. Look at the words and phrases that you could include in your essay. Discuss what they mean. How would you use them in your essay?

> convenience meal   processed food   high-energy drinks   sedentary lifestyles
> low nutritional value   bigger portions   kidney failure   suffer from heart attacks
> weight gain   overworked   a highly detrimental effect

5a Read the main body of an sample essay that answers question 2 in exercise 2a. Does the writer feel that the changes to diet is a positive or negative development?

Because of the increasing amount of time that many of us spend at work, there is little time to cook. This has led to convenience meals becoming more popular. Furthermore, long working hours also mean less sleep, so that many people resort to high sugar energy drinks to remain alert. In addition, long days increase the likelihood of our relaxing at home rather than doing active hobbies. This results in our adopting a more sedentary lifestyle. Research has found that those who eat dinner while watching TV will generally eat more food.

The changes to lifestyle described above can only be described as having a negative effect on diet and health. Convenience food tends to be high in sugar and fat and low in nutrients. It is likely that this poor diet will cause many people to develop diseases such as type two diabetes. Sufferers can also develop kidney failure and suffer from heart attacks as a result of the disease. A sedentary lifestyle and bigger portions of food will inevitably trigger weight gain, which will put a strain on an overweight person's heart, and other organs.

To sum up, lifestyle changes has led to overworked members of the population consuming processed convenience food, which can be high in sugar and fat and have low nutritional value. It is probable that this, coupled with our eating bigger quantities and food and moving less is likely to have a highly detrimental effect on our health.

5b Read the sample essay again. <u>Underline</u> expressions that introduce the result of a situation.

5c Complete the sentences with the expressions <u>underlined</u> in exercise 5b.

1 Less time spent being active can .... weight gain.

2 Eating late sometimes .... we suffer from indigestion at night.

3 Contracting type 2 diabetes .... of suffering a heart attack.

4 People work increasingly long hours these days. .... higher stress levels.

5 Obese people .... conditions such as diabetes.

6 High levels of stress can .... mental health problems.

✎ EXAM TASK

6 Work in pairs. Plan and write a response to the essay question.

> Due to improvements in healthcare, there is an increasing trend of people living longer in many countries around the world. In what ways has this affected the population as a whole? Do you think this is a positive or negative development?

Give reasons for your answer and include any relevant examples from your knowledge or experience. Write at least 250 words.

A change of plan

1   Work in pairs. Discuss the questions.

- How has it changed over the years? How do you think it will change in the future?
- How many international retailers can you think of which have branches in your local town or city?

2a   Look at the floor plans. What do they show? What tenses will you use to describe the changes depicted?

The diagrams below are existing and proposed floor plans for the redevelopment of a shopping complex.

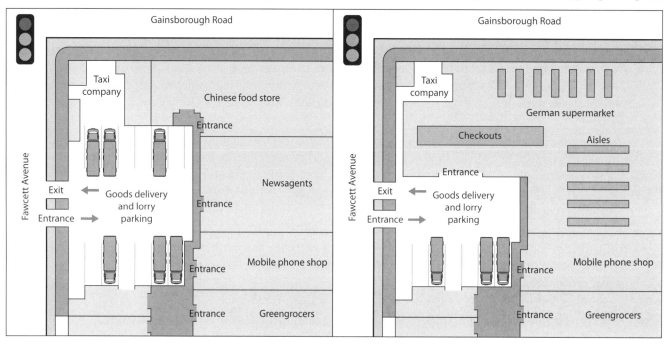

2b   Number the paragraphs of the sample sample so that they reflect the plan.

Plan:

1 Paraphrase the Task 1 question
2 Summarise the main changes to the complex
3 Paragraph describing the replacement of two stores with one
4 Paragraph describing change in footprint of store and internal space division

.... At present, a Chinese food store and newsagents **1**............................ (occupation) the north-east corner of the complex. However the plan is to **2**............................ (combination) the floor space of both stores, by **3**............................ (demolition) the dividing wall and **4**............................ (replacement) the existing stores with a German supermarket.

.... It is clear that significant changes will be made in terms of the number, type and size of shops and to the delivery and parking space. Two shops will be **5**............................ (replacement) by one and the parking space will be **6**............................ (reduction).

.... The footprint of the existing stores will also be **7**............................ (enlargement), to occupy space currently **8**............................ (dedication) to the lorry park. This will mean lorry parking space will be **9**............................ (half). Inside the supermarket, an open plan space will be **10**............................ (division) by aisles and checkouts will be **11**............................ (situation) near to the new entrance.

.... The first picture shows the current layout of a shopping complex, and the second shows some planned changes to its space and purpose.

2c Complete the sample diagram description with the correct verb form of the noun in brackets. Then check your answers in the key.

2d Read the sentences. Are they the same as sentences in the sample description in exercise 2b?

1 It is clear that significant changes will be made in terms of the number, type and size of shops and the delivery and parking space will change too.

2 However the plan is to combine the floor space of both stores, by demolishing the dividing wall and to replace the existing stores with a German supermarket.

3 Underline the part of each sentence that is not parallel. Then rewrite the sentence in parallel form.

1 The entrance has been expanded to avoid trolleys getting stuck and to avoid queues of people at the entrance at busy times.

2 Not only has the staircase been demolished and the door has been moved too.

3 Neither the function of the gallery or its basic floorplan has changed.

4 The disadvantages of having an open plan space is overcrowding in particular areas and the passengers become confused about the direction they should move in.

4 Work in pairs. Look at the pair of diagrams below and decide how you will structure your description.

✏ EXAM TASK

5 Write a description of the plans. Summarise the information by selecting and reporting the main features, and make comparisons where relevant. Write at least 150 words.

The diagrams below are existing and proposed floor plans for the redevelopment of an airport departure lounge.

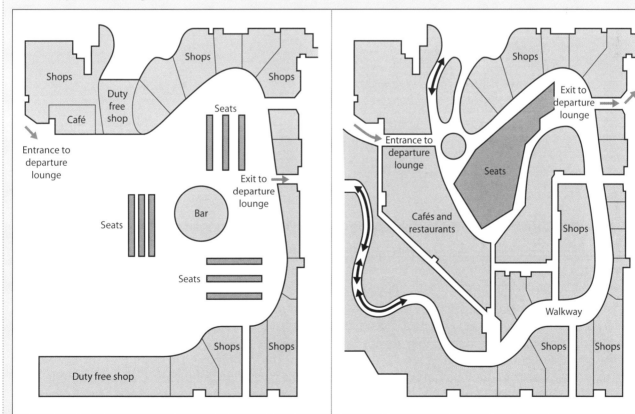

60 mins

Global village

1 **Work in pairs. Discuss how each of the photographs relates to the theme of globalisation. Do you feel the images are representative of our world today?**

2a **Read the essay question below. Brainstorm the benefits and drawbacks of globalisation. Use the following headings for the benefits: Business / Trade, Political relationships, Developing countries. Use the following headlines for the drawbacks: Cost of labour, Exploitation of employees Waste / Pollution.**

Over the past few decades, the world has become a global village where trade and communication are not restricted by borders between countries. Do the benefits of globalisation outweigh the drawbacks?

> **Exam tip**
>
> A word like globalisation can be spelt in two ways: *globalisation* (British English) and *globalization* (American English) The IELTS test recognises both American and British English in terms of spelling, grammar and choice of words. In general it's a good idea to stick to one spelling system.

2b **Correct the mistakes in the first two paragraphs of an IELTS candidate's essay.**

There has been said that the world has become a 'global village'; a place that people of all nationalities can communicate and trade without being limited by their country of origin. There are many advantages to this development and some disadvantages. This essay will examine both.

To examine the benefits first, business is becoming increasingly international and globalisation allows for everyone to communicate easily using a lingua franca: English. Their modes of communication are also globalized; email, phone and texts, they are not limited by borders and facilitate quick communication. The exchange of goods and services around the world means that people living in countries with limited resources can access goods who can significantly improve the its quality of life. It also encourages multi-nationals to invest in the workforce in developing countries, thereby creating employment in these. Trade between nations develops political understanding because countries benefit from one another's assets and forge trade agreements.

3a **Read the two paragraphs below. Which do you think is easier to read? Give reasons for your answer.**

A There are some disadvantages to globalisation. International businesses tend to move their businesses to a country where labour is cheap, and this often necessitates making employees redundant. When new employees in developing countries are taken on, it is sometimes at a very low wage and not with very favourable working conditions. Globalisation can affect the environment. People no longer buy and eat locally grown food or other products; they often consume goods which have been developed and grown abroad. Transporting products has led to an increase in pollution levels. The increase in production of food and crops also leads to a greater amount of industrial waste being produced and having to be disposed of because globalisation has meant that more food and crops have been produced to meet demand.

B On the other hand, there are some disadvantages to globalisation, for example, unemployment. International businesses tend to move their businesses to a country where labour is cheap, and this move often necessitates making existing employees redundant. When new employees in developing countries are taken on, it is sometimes at a very low wage and a new employee does not always enjoy very favourable working conditions. A further negative impact of globalisation is that it can affect the environment. With globalisation, people no longer buy and eat locally grown food or other products; they often consume goods which have been developed and grown abroad. Transporting these products has led to an increase in pollution levels. The increase in production of food and crops which results from an increase in consumption due to globalisation also leads to a greater amount of industrial waste being produced and having to be disposed of.

3b <u>Underline</u> **words and phrases in the paragraph you chose in exercise 3a which increases its cohesion.**

3c **Complete the concluding paragraph to the essay with the words in the box.**

> drawbacks   globalisation   however   it   it   its   these   whilst

In conclusion, **(1)** .... there are huge economic, social and political advantages to

globalisation, **(2)** .... also has environmental and ethical drawbacks. Some of

(3) ....**(4)** .... can be mitigated by tough international controls,

(5) .... On balance, I think that globalization is a good thing. **(6)** .... is

also impossible to put back the clocks and reverse the effect of **(7)** .... , so the best

approach is perhaps to try to reduce **(8)** .... disadvantages.

✏ EXAM TASK

4a **Plan and write a response to the exam task.**

> It has been said that it is difficult to notice the differences between countries nowadays. All over the world, people share the same brands, buy the same clothes and food and watch the same TV programmes. Do the advantages outweigh the disadvantages of this?

Give reasons for your answer and include any relevant examples from your own knowledge or experience. Write at least 250 words.

4b **Work in pairs. Swap your essay with your partner. Check your partner's essay for cohesion errors and make suggestions for improvements.**

Caught on camera

1a **Work in pairs. Discuss the questions.**

1 How many closed-circuit television (CCTV) cameras did you spot on your way to school today? Does their presence make you feel safe or irritated?

2 What is the purpose of CCTV cameras? Do you think they achieve this? Why / Why not?

3 What are the benefits and drawbacks of CCTV cameras?

1b **Read the short text below. How does it answer questions 2 and 3 in exercise 1a?**

Millions of closed-circuit television (CCTV) cameras are installed in city streets, car parks, businesses and in residences every year in order to cut crime and increase public safety. In the UK alone, there are over 2 million cameras and this number continues to rise. The impact of CCTV camera installations has been the subject of a number of studies which seek to assess their efficacy. Overall, it seems that their presence have both advantages and disadvantages. Benefits include the 'halo effect', which refers to the decrease in the amount of crimes committed in nearby CCTV-free areas. On the other hand, they can also lead to the 'displacement effect': the increased committal of crimes in areas where there aren't CCTV cameras.

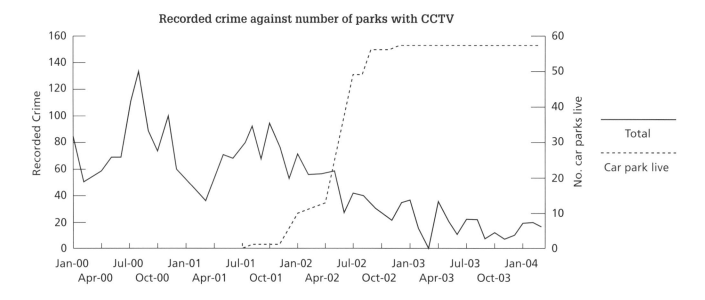

Recorded crime against number of parks with CCTV

2a **Look at the line graph and answer the questions.**

1 What type of crime do you think the CCTV cameras recorded?

2 What is the main correlation that can be seen in the chart? Complete this sentence:

Overall, we can see that as the number of car parks with live CCTV cameras increased

---

Exam tip

When you are concentrating on describing data in a graph, it is easy to make mistakes with verb forms and article use. In the exam, make sure that you leave time to check your work.

2b **Read the sample answer. What conclusion does the candidate reach about the efficacy of CCTV cameras?**

The line graph illustrates the number of crimes that were committed in <u>the</u> car parks over .... four year period, both a year before and three years after the introduction of <u>the</u> live CCTV cameras.

Overall, it can be seen that, as .... number of CCTV cameras installed increased, ... number of crimes committed decreased, although there <u>was</u> sharp rises and falls in <u>the</u> crime numbers throughout each year. Looking at the graph in more detail .... number of crimes peaked in July 2000, when just under 140 .... committed.

This number then fell sharply to .... low of 30 the following year, only to <u>picked</u> up again to approximately 90 crimes in July 2001, which was when the first CCTV camera was installed.

Shortly after that, in July 2002, when there were 20 CCTV <u>camera</u>, ... number of crimes had fallen to 60. Thereafter, when .... number of cameras was almost <u>triple</u> to 58 in January 2003, the crime rate dipped to .... zero. Althoughit did rise sharply to 40 crimes over .... next few months, it continued to be low and didn't surpass 10 crimes for .... remainder of 2003.

3a **Look at the gaps. Which types of words are missing? What type of mistakes are <u>underlined</u>?**

3b **Work in pairs. Correct the mistakes that the candidate has made with articles. Use the usage notes in the box to help you.**

> We don't use an article when we refer to a plural noun in general.
>
> We use the indefinite article (a or an) when we refer to a singular noun and the noun is one thing out of many.
>
> We use the definite article (the) to refer to a specific thing that the reader knows about.

3c **Correct the <u>underlined</u> errors in the sample answer.**

✏ EXAM TASK

4 **Write a description of the table. Summarise the information by selecting and reporting the main features, and make comparisons where relevant. Write at least 150 words within 40 minutes**

Changes in recorded crime in CCTV systems 2016–2018			
Scheme	No. of crimes committed pre CCTV	No. of crimes committed after CCTV	Change in crime rate (%)
City suburbs	1,526	1,098	-28
CCTV in car parks	794	214	-73
Cambrook	5,106	4,584	-10
Shirehill	352	338	-4
Marham	245	290	18
North Borough	334	335	0.3
Council Estate	112	101	-10

Causes of crime

1a   **Match the definitions (a–g) to the topic vocabulary in bold.**

1 People who exhibit **anti-social behaviour** such as using abusive language, joyriding and dropping litter should be punished with a short **prison sentence**.

2 Prison doesn't stop criminals from **re-offending**.

3 There is often a **high incidence** of crime in areas where there is a high level of poverty.

4 **White-collar criminals** should not **serve a custodial sentence** in the same prisons as those who have committed **serious crimes**.

a) a large or frequent number of things happening in a particular place or situation

b) committing crime more than once

c) a way of acting that is likely to cause alarm or distress to other people

d) criminals who commit office or business related crime such as fraud

e) spend time in prison

f) the amount of time a criminal is told that they have to spend in prison

g) crimes such as murder, drug-trafficking, arson, kidnapping

Exam tip

When learning topic vocabulary for use in your Task 2 essays, try to learn the words that the particular item 'collocates' or goes together with. For example, rather than learning 'anti-social behaviour', learn 'to exhibit anti-social behaviour'.

1b   **Work in pairs. Discuss whether you agree with statements 1–4 in exercise 1a. Give reasons for your answers.**

2a   **Read the essay question. What type of essay does it require the candidate to write?**

> Many criminals re-offend after they have spent time in prison. Why is there such a high number of criminals who re-offend, and what measures can be taken to tackle this problem?

2b   **Work in small groups. Brainstorm a list of problems and solutions in response to the essay question in exercise 3a.**

2c   **Read the sample essay and complete the plan with ideas from the essay.**

Problems:

1 Criminals choose a life of crime because they feel they have no other choice

2 Criminals have often had an .... and haven't been educated: a lack of

.... = no means to earn money

3 Poverty leads to a criminal committing crimes and ending up in prison

4 Prison doesn't help: it brings a first-time offender into contact with other .... who can be a

.... Also makes it difficult for a criminal to find a .... on release

Solutions:

5 An education can be provided while the criminal is in prison: e.g. ....

6 ....: brings prisoner into contact with his / her local community = encourages

them to value the community / dissuades them from damaging it

7 Practical help to find .... and ....

It is a commonly known fact that a prison sentence does not necessarily reform a criminal. This essay will explore the reasons for this and suggest steps that could be taken to avoid criminals re-offending.

Criminals often turn to crime because they feel that they have no other choice. They are often had **1** <u>an unhappy time during childhood</u> and are sometimes deprived of the opportunity to gain qualifications and therefore to earn money legally. Once a criminal is serving **2** <u>time in prison for committing a crime</u>, they will inevitably come into contact with other criminals, many of whom can influence **3** <u>a person who has only offended once</u> negatively. Even if a prisoner wants to live **4** <u>life without committing a crime again</u> when they are released, it is difficult to do so as a **5** <u>history of having committed a crime</u> makes it challenging to find a job.

There are, however, ways that the criminal justice system can help criminals avoid **6** <u>committing another crime, ending up in prison and then committing further crimes on release, and so on</u>. For instance, they can provide the prisoner with vocational training, so that an inmate can enter into **7** <u>trades that would be suitable for them when they get out of prison</u>. Another way of reducing the number of **8** <u>criminals who commit crimes repeatedly</u> is to avoid sending them to prison at all. Community service will underline **9** <u>why a community is valuable</u> to a criminal and dissuade them from doing any more damage to it.

In conclusion, despite the fact that there are many understandable reasons why criminals continue to follow a life of crime, there are **10** <u>many ways of stopping criminals from offending again</u>, ranging from equipping prisoners with useful life skills, to encouraging them to help in the community.

3a Match the <u>underlined</u> phrases in the sample essay with one of the noun phrases.

a) an unhappy childhood ....

b) a community's value ....

c) a crime-free life ....

d) criminal record ....

e) custodial sentence ....

f) first-time offender ....

g) suitable trades on release ....

h) repeat offenders ....

i) solution to this situation ....

j) the vicious circle of reoffending ....

3b Match the noun phrases in exercise 3a with the patterns below.

1 (article +) adjective+noun ....

2 (adjective +) noun + prepositional phrase ....

3 (compound) noun+ noun ....

3c Work in pairs. Discuss which improves the coherence and readability of the essay a) the original essay b) the essay with the noun phrases from exercise 3a. Give reasons for your answer.

Exam tip

Academic texts typically feature a high proportion of nouns and noun phrases. Noun phrases allow the writer to express a lot of information concisely. Use noun phrases in your Task 2 essay.

✎ EXAM TASK

4 Plan and write a response to the exam task.

> It is often thought that the increase in juvenile crime can be attributed to violence in the media. What do you think is the reason for a growth in the rate of juvenile crime? What solutions can you offer to deal with this situation?

Give reasons for your answer and include any relevant examples from your own knowledge or experience. Write at least 250 words.

60 mins

Social trends

1a **Choose one of the following options.**

1 Draw a bar graph that shows how much time you have spent on social media sites every day this week.

2 Draw a line graph that shows which time you are most active on social media during a 24 hour period.

1b **Find a partner who chose the same option as you in exercise 1a. Describe the most significant pieces of data in your graph to your partner. Are there similarities between your graphs? Name the tense that you used to describe your graph to your partner. Do you think it was the correct tense to use?**

2a **Look at the graph below. Which age and gender used social media the most? Are you surprised by this? Why / Why not?**

The bar graph illustrates social networking usage in the UK between 2008 and 2015. The data is broken down by gender and by age.

Social networking usage by gender and age 2008–2015, GB

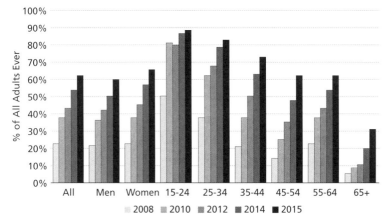

2b **Read a sample introduction to a description of the graph in exercise 2a. Why would the candidate lose marks? Replace words in the introduction with alternatives from the box.**

> by age group   by sex   over a seven year period   the percentage of adults   who visited social networking sites

2c **Complete the rest of the graph description with verbs in the box in the correct tense.**

> (not) be (x3)   follow   increase   reach   rise   see   spend   use

Overall, we can see that the percentage of adults using social media sites **1**......................... between 2008 and

2015 from around 20% to approximately 60% in 2015. It can also be observed that social networking

2......................... most popular with people of 15–24 years old.

Looking at the details, we can see that in 2008, an almost equal percentage of men and women

3......................... social media. In the years that **4**........................., however, a slightly higher percentage

of women **5**......................... time on social media and this difference between genders **6**.........................

a peak in 2015, at around 8%.

There **7**......................... also a significant difference in adults of different ages using social media,

particularly between 2008 and the rest of the years. With social media users of between 15 and 24 years

of age, there **8**......................... such a difference between 2010 and 2014; overall, the percentage of

users **9**......................... by roughly 10%. This **10**......................... the only age group for which the

percentage of users **11**......................... by around 2% between 2010 and 2012; all the other age groups

12......................... a consistent rise in social media users of between 10 and 20 % year on year.

3a Imagine the year is 2018. Look at the graph. How many tenses would you use to describe the data?

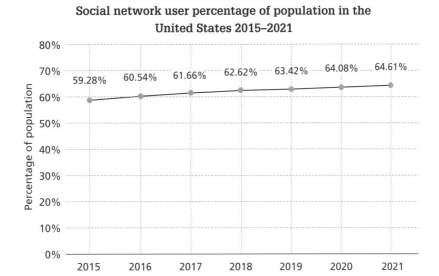

Social network user percentage of population in the United States 2015–2021

3b Choose the verb form that describes the data in the graph most accurately.

1 There has been / was a slight rise of around 3% in the percentage of people using social media sites since 2015.

2 In 2015, the percentage of social media users in the US has been / was at its lowest, at 59.28%.

3 The growth in social media penetration is predicted / is estimated to slow down between 2020 and 2021, when it is bound to / is thought to be likely to grow by only 1% as opposed to 2% between the other years.

4 It is going to / it is probable that the percentage of the adult population using social media will continue / is continuing to grow between 2018 and 2021.

> **Exam tip**
>
> Certain future forms are appropriate when you describe future trends. The passive voice is often useful to show that the data in the graph is only predicted e.g. *It is probable that.*

✏ EXAM TASK

4 Imagine the year is currently 2018. Write a description of the graph. Summarise the information by selecting and reporting the main features, and make comparisons where relevant. Write at least 150 words.

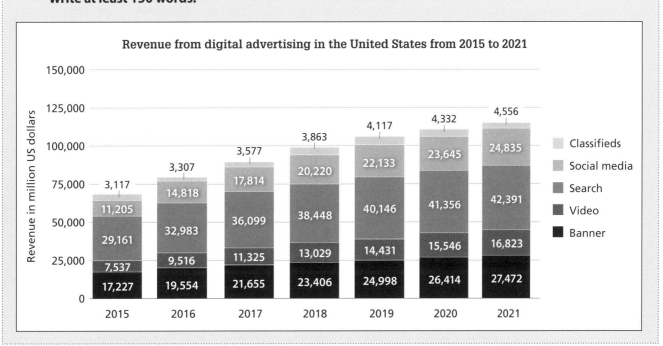

Revenue from digital advertising in the United States from 2015 to 2021

Spreading the news

1 **Work in pairs. Discuss the questions.**

1 Can you give examples of a tabloid and a broadsheet newspaper in your country?

2 If you read the news, do you prefer to do so with a print newspaper or online?

3 Do you ever get your news from social media sites? Do you consider them to be reliable sources?

4 Which of these terms describing journalists does not have negative connotations?
  a) a hack   **b)** the gutter press   **c)** the paparazzi   **d)** the press

5 Explain the difference between the following terms:
  1 a) news coverage   **b)** news bulletins   **c)** news flash
  2 a) edition   **b)** circulation   **c)** readership

2a **Read the exam task below. Is it possible to partially agree with the statement? Why / Why not?**

> Although an increasing number of people read news on the Internet, newspapers will continue to be the most important source of news. Do you agree or disagree?

2b **Read the example essay below. How has the candidate written a balanced answer?**

In recent years, there has been a growth in the percentage of the population who get their news online. Despite this, many people believe that newspapers will continue to dominate as the primary source of news. This essay disagrees with this view and makes an alternative prediction.

There are a number of reasons why newspapers are likely to become only one of the many sources of news. Firstly, they are inconvenient; one needs to leave the house to buy one and **1 having done** so, it is time-consuming for the consumer to find a story, due to the number of different supplements **2 comprising** a newspaper. Secondly, **3 by being** printed once a day only, they cannot be updated. Furthermore, in this age of **4 user-generated** content, it seems out-of-date that there is no way for the reader to react to newspaper stories. Finally, many of the stories **5 published** will feel irrelevant to particular individuals.

In contrast, internet based news is convenient to access and more relevant, due to it being easier to read them selectively. Frequently updated stories feel dynamic and having read a story, it is straightforward to post opinions online. For all these reasons, I believe that online newspapers will become as important as print newspapers. However, they are unlikely to completely replace print newspapers for a few reasons. Firstly, the older generation, used to traditional news sources, may well prefer to read printed news. Secondly, the readership of online newspapers currently enjoying their news for free may well be put off doing so should they be required to pay.

In conclusion, while printed papers are likely to decline in popularity due to their various drawbacks compared to their online equivalents, I believe they will remain a viable source of news.

2c **Match the participle forms in bold in the first paragraph of the sample essay to their description.**

A A past participle that is part of a reduced relative passive clause e.g. many of the celebrity stories that are published today will be forgotten tomorrow.

B A past participle that works like an adjective and is positioned before a noun.

C A perfect participle that shows that one action takes place before the action of the main verb.

D A present participle that follows a preposition.

E A present participle that that is part of a reduced relative clause e.g. people who use using social media sites to get their news are unlikely to gain an in-depth understanding of a story.

2d **Find examples of participle forms that match uses A–E in exercise 2c in the final paragraphs of the sample essay.**

✎ EXAM TASK

3a **Read the exam task and part of a sample response below. Does the candidate agree or disagree?**

> Newspapers have an enormous influence on people's opinions and ideas. Some people believe that this influence is predominantly negative. Do you agree or disagree?

Give reasons for your answer and include any relevant examples from your own knowledge or experience. Write at least 250 words.

3b **Replace the words in bold with perfect, present and past participles.**

There are many reasons why a newspaper's influence can be detrimental to a reader's understanding of a situation. Firstly, newspapers tend to be politically-biased and so report a story from a particular perspective, **which can prevent** a person from forming **an opinion that is independent and well-informed**. As well as **presenting a view that is distorted**, newspapers will select stories based on whether they will help to sell the newspaper, rather than featuring stories **that are worthy of being featured. This means that the reader may be left ignorant** of important events **that are happening around the world**.

Now that I have outlined the disadvantages of newspapers, I should say that a lot depends on **a person's choice** of a suitable newspaper. In other words, it is possible to choose a source of news that reports stories responsibly.

3c **Plan and write your response to the exam task.**

Exam tip

Using participle clauses in your essays can make your writing more concise, which will allow you to write complex, accessible sentences and improve your band score.

WRITING

WRITING TASK 1

You should spend about 20 minutes on this task.

> *The diagram below shows the movement of carbon in its different forms around the natural environment.*
>
> *Summarise the information by selecting and reporting the main features, and make comparisons where relevant.*

Write at least 150 words.

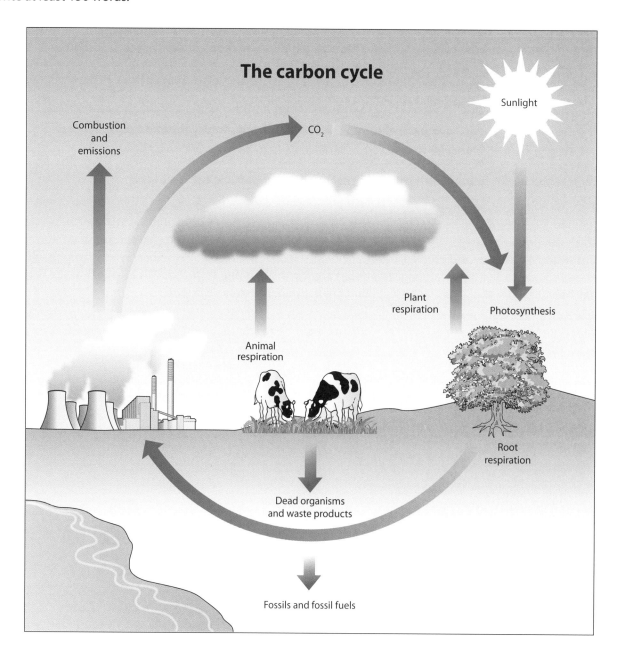

WRITING TASK 2

You should spend about 40 minutes on this task.

Write about the following topic:

Some people think that it is better to educate boys and girls in separate schools. Others, however, believe that boys and girls benefit more from attending mixed schools. Discuss both views and give your opinion.

Give reasons for your answer and include any relevant examples from your own knowledge or experience.

Write at least 250 words.

IELTS Writing Answer Sheet – TASK 1

Candidate Name

Centre Number

Candidate Number

Module (shade one box):　　Academic ▭　　　General Training ▭

Test date

D　D　　M　M　　Y　Y　Y　Y

TASK 1

Do not write below this line

100913/2

SAMPLE

Do not write below this line

OFFICIAL USE ONLY

Candidate Number: [   ]   TA [ ] CC [ ] LR [ ] GRA [ ]

Examiner 2 Number: [   ]

Underlength	No. of words	Penalty		Off-topic	Memorised	Illegible

Candidate Number: [   ]   TA [ ] CC [ ] LR [ ] GRA [ ]

Examiner 1 Number: [   ]

Underlength	No. of words	Penalty		Off-topic	Memorised	Illegible

Answers

English as an additional language (pages 6–7)

1a English as an additional language is a term used for when English is not the first language spoken. Students' own answers.

1b India: over 125 million, Pakistan: over 92 million, Phillipines: over 89 million, Nigeria: over 79 million, Germany: over 46 million, United States: over 42 million, Bangladesh: over 29 million, Egypt: over 28 million, France: over 23 million, China: over 10 million

2a 1 Students' own answers.
2 a specific point of time: 2011
3 numbers
4 the past simple
5 Students' own answers.
6 Students' own answers.

2b Students' own answers.

2c 1 highest 2 most common 3 fewer 4 lower 5 fewer 6 fewest 7 higher

2d a) slightly, marginally b) far c) comparable to d) compared to around double the number

3a B
The writer uses respectively to refer two sets of numbers back to two different types of speakers. Respectively makes it clear that the numbers are in the same order as the types of speakers. Thus we know that there are 220 thousand Bengali speakers and 215 thousand Gujarati speakers.

3b Overall, we can see that the highest number of proficient Spanish speakers arrived in the US between 2004 and 2009. We can also see that during this time, there were far higher numbers of advanced Spanish speakers from Spain than there were Spanish speakers from Mexico, with around 366,000 and more than 200,000 respectively in 2004 and 2006, and between 2007 and 2009.

4a Students' own answers.

4b **Sample answer**

The bar graph compares the number of proficient English speakers arriving in the UK between the years 1961 and 2011, by their country of origin.

Overall, we can see that the highest number of proficient English speakers arrived in England and Wales between 2004 and 2009. We can also see that during this time, there were far higher numbers of advanced English speakers from Europe than there were from the Middle East. Between 2004 and 2006, and between 2007 and 2009, there were 216,000 and nearly 150,000 more proficient European speakers of English respectively.

There was a similarly large difference before 1961. Conversely, for the remainder of the years, there was a higher number of proficient English speakers originating from the Middle East and Asia than from Europe. The years between 1971 and 1980 saw the biggest difference, with almost 140,000 speakers of English from the Middle East and Asia.

The years between 1991 and 1996 saw the lowest number of proficient English speakers arrive in England and Wales from both Europe and the Middle East and Asia, with around 100,000 arriving from the former and between 80 and 90,000 from the latter.

Saving languages (pages 8–9)

1a 3,000 years ago was when Cherokee was thought first to be spoken, 6,000 languages in the world are imperilled, top ten languages today are spoken by 50% of the population

1b Students' own answers.

1c **A** b) **B** a)

1d a) B b) A

2a a) A b) B c) B

2b

Advantages	Disadvantages
3 makes tourism easier: everyone can understand one another	NOT USED leads to a lack of understanding of the arts: great works such as the Iliad were not written down until very recently. Some that are never written down might be lost forever
4 enables everyone to access and understand diverse cultures: literary works from different cultures translated into a single language.	**7** leads to a loss of knowledge about a place: e.g. Amazonian languages tell us about the rainforest
1 facilitates globalisation: business is easier and cheaper to do with a common language.	**5** leads to loss of cultural identity: language defines a particular people and their sense of self
2 cheaper: translation becomes unnecessary	**6** leads to loss of particular words: some words are particular to a language e.g. oo-kah-huh-sdee (Cherokee) (cute, gorgeous, delight, engendering a desire to squeeze something – the feeling when you see a kitten)

2c dying out, exclusive, benefits and drawbacks

2d **convenience:** convenient, easily, useful, removes difficulties, simpler, readily
loss: considerable price to pay, loss, impoverishment, disappears forever

3 **Sample answer**

It is a commonly known fact that many languages are on the verge of extinction because few people speak them. Some people feel that the responsibility for saving these languages lies with the government, while others feel that public money should be spent elsewhere. This essay will consider both of these perspectives.

Saving a language is, without doubt, a worthwhile endeavour. It prevents cultures from dying out and preserves words and knowledge which are unique to diversity. It is expensive to save a language as teachers need to be found and trained and resources need to be created.
It makes sense that some government funding is invested in this endeavour as language is part of a country's identity.

However, we need to bear in mind that saving a language is largely an academic exercise. Even if people learn the language, it is unlikely that rare languages will be used in everyday situations; the most widely known language will be used. Therefore, it is probable that the language will remain in classroom materials and books predominantly. If rare languages are preserved in books, academics and language specialists will have the opportunity to study the languages in the future and uncover any 'lost' knowledge.

In conclusion, on the one hand, saving a language preserves cultural uniqueness and knowledge but on the other, it is only possible to save it in an academic sense, rather than enable its everyday widespread use. As the saving of a language is limited, it makes sense to use a limited amount of government money to this end.

Location is everything (pages 10–11)

1a Students' own answers.
1b Students' own answers.

2a In relation to the city: S1 is in the city centre and S2 is to the North-West of the city centre. In relation to the transport links: S1 is near the railway line which leads to Bishopgate. S2 is in close proximity to the roads leading to Honston, Cambrook and Great Bardon.
2b **A**3 **B**1 **C**2 **D**4
2c **a)** whereas, however, conversely, on the other hand
b) particularly because the complex at S1 would be located in a pedestrian zone as there isn't a main road from this town towards the out of town complex
Because of the proximity of S1 to a railway line

Due to the fact that it would be accessible to residents
c) which is a no traffic zone
that a leisure complex in town would bring about who could reach the complex by car or bus making parking and access difficult
that the line passes through Bishopgate
2d **1** which would, **2** Conversely, **3** because it is situated, **4** On the other hand, **5** who

3a Students' own answers.
3b Possible answers: shopping mall / potential locations
3c **Sample answer**

The map shows two potential locations for a shopping mall in Long Melling. The first location (S1) is in the centre of town, whereas the second location (S2) is in the suburbs, in a green space.

From the point of view of the residents of Long Melling, S1 would be more conveniently located as it would be within walking distance of all the residential areas and close to other shops. Conversely, S2 would be more difficult for many of the residents to reach and they may not appreciate a shopping centre being located in one of their green spaces.

The location of S2, on the other hand, is better for the residents of the large town of Hitchin, who can access it from the main road, or by coming into the railway station by train. However, for the residents of Chatterfield, which is a smaller town, S2 would be difficult to reach as they would have to drive across town, which could bring about traffic congestion.

Although both locations have benefits and drawbacks, on balance I would recommend locating the shopping centre in S1, for the benefit of the residents of Long Melling and Chatterfield.

The wrong move? (pages 12–13)

1a Students' own answers.
1b **A** city life: 'concrete jungles'
air pollution
developed infrastructure
good education resources
high cost of living
homelessness and poverty
higher stress levels
modern transportation links
overpopulation sense of anonymity traffic congestion
B rural life: laid-back, slow pace of life
limited career prospects
peaceful
sparsely populated
tightly-knit communities
locally cultivated, organic food

2 **1** a) **2** b)

3a Nowadays, an increasing number of people are choosing to move to cities. However, living in cities has a number of drawbacks. There are many issues associated with metropolitan living. For example, …

3b Suggested answer: c)

3c 1 c 2 a 3 b

4a 1 Without doubt, it is the duty of the government to address these issues. Only the government has the power to change laws so that more land is made available for housing.

2 In my view, this is a very regrettable situation. I don't feel it is right that there is such an inequality in the standard of living.

In my opinion, the onus of solving this disparity in living standards is on the government.

4b a live b houses c an increase d low earners e responsibility / onus f introduce legislation g economical h provision i disparity j to address / to solve k regrettable situation l a lack

5 **Sample answer**

The existence of large firms and industries in city centres undoubtedly creates housing shortages and congestion, as employees generally live in the same city as their place of work and need to travel to it. It has been argued that relocating industries to the countryside would solve these issues. In my opinion, however, doing so will actually create further problems.

Relocating industries to rural areas will not solve a problem outright, it will simply move it. For example, moving industry may well ease rush-hour congestion in the city centre, but it will also create congestion on minor rural roads, as commuters try to reach their place of work. This congestion is likely to be worse than that found in the city centre as traffic will not be as easily diverted. In addition to traffic congestion and associated pollution, rural areas will be blighted by fumes given off by the industries that have been moved there.

It is risky to assume that by moving industries outside the city, employees will also relocate. They may find it more convenient to remain in the city, where other facilities such as schools can be found. Thus, the housing shortage in city centres are unlikely to be solved just by moving industries and factories.

To sum up, moving industries to rural areas will not only cause environmental damage to the countryside, but it is unlikely to solve housing issues within the city centre. For this reason, I would argue that relocating large companies and factories to rural areas was unadvisable.

How much sleep do you need? (pages 14–15)

1 Students' own answers.

2a 1 2012–2013, 2011–2012 2 four 3 10, 11

2b Students' own answers.

2c 2b, 3c

3a a) more b) percentages c) past simple

3b b)

3c 1 slight, steady, significant, concurrent
2 markedly, dramatically, marginally
3 relatively

3d the words 'there was'
big change: significant, markedly, dramatically
small change: slight, marginally, relatively

4b **Sample answer**

The graph illustrates the changes in sleep duration experienced by adults of 15–19 years old in the years between 2003 and 2013.

In general, we can see that sleep duration was highest at weekends, and the percentage of young adults accruing more than nine hours of sleep increased markedly between 2009 and 2013. In addition, we can also see that the overall percentage of sleep duration increased.

Although the percentage of young adults getting 9 hours' sleep or more on weekdays remained relatively consistent, with slight fluctuations, those adults reporting fewer than seven hours' sleep on weekdays fell steadily from a peak of 20 percent in 2004 to a low of 12 in 2012.

There was a steady rise in weekend sleep duration to a high in 2013 of 82% of young adults who were getting more than nine hours per night. There was a concurrent decrease in the percentage of adults getting less than nine hours' sleep at weekends over the same period.

Education matters (pages 16–17)

1a Students' own answers.

1b 1 2 2 3 3 1

1c Students' own answers.

1d 2(TG), 1 (TS) or 3 (JR)

2a **Paragraph 1**
1 c) 2 a) 3 d) 4 b)
Paragraph 2
1 b) 2 d) 3 a) 4 c)

2b a) Not only, but b) consequently c) On the other hand d) instead e) in turn f) Therefore

2c 1 As a result 2 instead 3 Not only 4 but

3a Students' own answers.

3b   Sample answer

Whether students' time is better spent studying arts and humanities subjects rather than science and mathematics is a widely-debated issue. In my view, the answer depends very much on a student's age and career ambitions. This essay will expand on this view.

Up to a student's mid-teens, I believe that a well-balanced education is important. It is very difficult to argue that one subject is more important than another at this stage; each has its own merits. For example, history gives a student an appreciation of events that have shaped their present situation, a study of literature instills an appreciation and understanding of language and literary heritage. Art develops critical thinking, motor skills and aesthetic sense. Science is fundamental in our understanding of how systems and organisms in the world work and maths equips us with reasoning and practical skills.

However, when a student reaches an age at which they start to make career decisions, it makes more sense that they specialise in the types of subjects that might help them to achieve their ambitions. For instance, if they wish to study architecture at university, art may be more useful to them than science. Conversely, a knowledge of mathematics is essential for potential engineering students.

To sum up, to argue that one subject is more worthy of study than another would be to oversimplify a complex issue. All subjects have their own uses and it's only when students start making decisions about their careers that it makes sense to study some subjects in favour of others.

The age–wage gap (pages 18–19)

1a   Students' own answers.

1b   Students' own answers.

2a   **a)** The table shows the median wage per week in 2015 of employees of different types.
b) In general, we can see that, for both full-time and part-time employees in 2015, salaries were lowest at ages 16– 17, and peaked when the employee reached 20–39 for full-time employees, and 40 – 49 for part-time employees.
c) 20–39 for full-time employees, and 40 – 49 for part-time employees.
d) yes, see answer c
e) If we compare genders, we can see that male employees earned much more than female employees earned.
f) We can see an exception to the gender wage gap in part-time workers.
g) The greatest gap in wages for full-time employees was between male and female workers of between 50 and 59. In contrast, the wage difference was greater for part-time employees

earlier on, between the ages of 16 and 17. The wage difference was greater between the ages of 16 and 17. It was also much less; at about £7 per week.

2b   See answers to exercise 2a.
A The table shows the median wage per week in 2015 of employees of different types.
B In general, we can see that, for both full-time and part-time employees in 2015, salaries were lowest at ages 16–17, and peaked when the employee reached 20–39 for full-time employees, and 40–49 for part-time employees. After these ages, earning capacity got lower, with both full-time male and female employees of 60 years plus earning around £100 per week less than an employee of 40 to 50 years old.
C If we compare genders, we can see that male employees earned much more than female employees earned. The greatest gap in wages for full-time employees was between male and female workers of between 50 and 59. In contrast, the wage difference was greater for part-time employees earlier on, between the ages of 16 and 17. The wage difference was greater between the ages of 16 and 17. It was also much less; at about £7 per week.
D We can see an exception to the gender wage gap in part-time workers. In contrast to their full time female employees, from the age of 20 to 60, female part-time employees actually earned more than male part-time employees.

2c   **a)** yes **b)** yes **c)** yes **d)** yes

3a   Students could delete: 'in wages' line 4; between the ages of 16 and 17 (penultimate line); We could replace 'The difference in wages (penultimate line) with 'It'.

3b   The table shows the median **salary** per week in 2015 of different types of workers.

Overall, **we can see that**, for all employees in 2015, salaries were lowest at ages 16–17, and peaked when the **wage earner** reached 20–39 for **full-time employees**, and 40–49 for **part-timers**. After these ages, earning capacity got **lower**, with both full-time male and female **employees** of 60 years plus bringing home around £100 per week **less** than a **worker** of 40 to 50 years old. **If we compare** genders, **we can notice that** male employees earned **considerably more** than their female **counterparts**. The greatest gap in wages for full-timers was between male and female workers of between 50 and 59. **By contrast**, the wage inequality was **greater** for part-timers earlier on, between the ages of 16 and 17. It was also **significantly less**; at about £7 per week. The exception to the gender wage discrepancy **can be observed** in part-time workers. **In contrast** to their full time **opposite numbers**, from the age of 20 to 60, women working part-time **earned** more than men doing the same.

3c   Students' own answers.

4 **Sample answers**

PAIR A

The table shows the median earnings before tax per annum for employees in 2015 in eight different countries.

Overall, we can see that male employees employed on a full-time basis earned a great deal more than their female counterparts.

The gender wage gap was greatest in the UAE, where men earned three and a half times more than women on average. The gap in Qatar was nearly as large, where men earn three times as much. The median annual wage in Qatar is also the highest of all, with men earning in excess of 100,000 dollars. Male employees in China earned far less than those in the Middle Eastern countries but still earned twice as much as women working in China.

The country with the smallest difference in wages between men and women was Vietnam, where the gap was around one thousand pounds. This was also the country where both genders had the lowest wages with women earning circa five thousand dollars and men earning approximately six thousand.

PAIR B

The table shows the number of senior and management roles occupied by both genders in a variety of different countries in 2015. In the majority of countries, we can see that the number of men in management positions outnumbered the number of women.

The difference between the number of senior male employees and female managers was greatest in the UAE, where there were nine times more male managers. Coming a close second was the UAE, where there were over seven times male managers to females, at 88 and 12 respectively.

In the majority of the other countries, there were around double the number of men employed in senior positions to the number of women, with the exception of Vietnam and China; the former having three times more men in management and the latter four times.

The only country where there were more women in senior positions than men was in the Philippines and there the difference in number was quite small, with roughly ten more female managers than male.

Stiff competition (pages 20–21)

1 Students' own answers.

2 Students' own answers. Suggestions: a) a younger employee: need to be trained up ambitious and single-minded conversant with new technologies highly qualified innovative and willing to take risks a lack of work experience more flexible with their time

b) an older employee: brings a sense of perspective committed to accuracy dependable and punctual expensive to make redundant generous with their time and expertise

3a Students' own answers

3b a) A b) A c) A d) B e) B f) B g) A

3c B

4a Students' own answers.

4b **1** b **2** c **3** a

4c a one-sided argument

4d Students could underline: For one thing, their training costs tend to be negligible as they are highly experienced in their field. Then there's the argument that they are often willing to work part-time, which makes them a cheaper proposition. In addition, older employees benefit the economy because they are directly contributing to it.

5a Students' own answers.

5b **Sample answer**

Many people consider the different characteristics of men and women to make each gender a better match for particular roles. This essay argues that one's suitability for a job cannot be determined by one's gender.

From an early age, gender stereotyping plays a part in determining the routes that boys and girls take in education and later careers. Society's expectations, TV shows and adverts teach us that women are more nurturing than men and so are more naturally suited to jobs that involve caring for others, such as nannies, or that they are suited to jobs that are more artistic, such as hairdressing or interior design. Despite the predominance of women in these professions, there is also a sufficient number of successful male nannies, interior designers and hairdressers to disprove the perception that women are somehow better at these jobs. The same applies to women in roles that are perceived as traditionally male.

What is more, it is an oversimplification to divide characteristics up by gender. An individual's personality is determined by a variety of factors such as genes, upbringing and education and there is a huge range of personalities within each gender. Likewise, there are a huge range of physiques; physically strong women exist, just as men with slight builds do. All of this means that it is the individual who is suited to a particular profession irrespective of their gender.

In conclusion, it is a huge simplification to say that one gender is better suited to a profession than another and we need to learn to ignore social stereotypes that lead people to form this opinion.

Urbanisation and development (pages 22–23)

1 Students' own answers.

2a **1** enlarge, expand, extend **2** cut down, demolish, knock down, pull down, remove **3** build, construct, erect, introduce, replace **4** convert, industrialise, make into, modernise, transform, turn into, urbanise **5** redevelop

2b enlargement, expansion, extension, demolition, removal, building, construction, erection, introduction, replacement, conversion, industrialisation, odernisation, transformation, urbanisation, redevelopment

2c Students' own answers.

3a **a)** Three. The biggest period of development was between 1990 and 2010.
b) population growth
c) as population grew, the town was developed and roads and railways were built

3b Answers in bold:
The map shows the urbanisation of the seaside resort town of Ki Pham Pham over a period of over **forty years**.
Initially, between 1977 and 1985, development was modest and concentrated along the coastline. However, between 1977 and 1990, there was a population explosion, with the number of residents in the area going up more than **twofold** *from 30,000 to* **60,000.** *As a consequence, the residential areas* **increased in** *size significantly. In addition, main roads and a railway were constructed to service the new developments.*
The first **decade** *of the 21st century saw even more development as the population continued to grow, increasing to 95,000 by* **2010**. *New residential areas transformed the appearance of the coastline as they were built along its stretch. Furthermore, a motorway was constructed to serve the area and as a result, more residential areas were built around it, to the north of the beachfront.*
Further changes that took place were the **modernisation of** *the waterpark on the beachfront and the renovation of the pier in* **2015.**

3c **a)** chronological **b)** causes, results **c)** paragraphs, periods **d)** main trends, end

4a **a)** 3 **b)** 2 **c)** 5 **d)** 6 **e)** 4 **f)** 1

4b **1** The map illustrates the expansion of the town of Wotton-End over a period of ten years.
2 As the industrial area grew, a shopping centre was built.
3 A bus route was constructed to help children to get to school.
4 The residential area was built on the green 'belt' surrounding the city. As a consequence, a copse of trees had to be cut down.
5 The residential area increased in this period, doubling in size.

6 The cinema was demolished with a new one built to the north of the old one.
7 In 1800, there was a housing crisis in the area. As a result, the number of residents decreased from 1 million to 500,000.

5a Students' own answers.
5b **Sample answer**
The maps illustrate developments in the village of Wotten-End between 1925 and 2015. Overall, it can be seen that, in response to an increase in population, facilities and infrastructure in the village have developed.

Between 1925 and 2015, the population of Wotten-End more than doubled, from 1,500 to 3,250 residents. Whilst the basic structure of the village remained unchanged, there was an increase in the number of houses built along the main streets of the village. Additional minor roads leading onto the main roads were also constructed, along with the new housing.

Existing facilities also expanded. For example, the secondary school increased in size and a main road was constructed outside the town to accommodate the growth in residential traffic. In addition, the existing small shops were replaced with one large supermarket. A large house was also converted into a supermarket. However, the post office remained unchanged. Finally, a leisure centre was built on the outskirts of the village, which could be reached by the new main road.

International travel (pages 24–25)

1 Students' own answers.

2a B
2b Students' own answers.
2c **1**F, **2**C, **3**D, **4**A, **5**G, **6**B, **7**E
2d **1** Culturally speaking
2 Economically speaking
3 From, point of view
4 Without, drawbacks
5 potentially negative impact

3a/b Linkers to show similar additional ideas**:** Also, what is more, **furthermore in addition, yet** Linkers to show contrasting ideas**:** However, although, on the other hand, **besides, despite, even though**, **in contrast, nevertheless**, **nonetheless, though**

3c **1 Despite understanding** the environmental drawbacks of flying, tourists continue to travel abroad.
2 Although thousands of tourists visit The Taj Mahal annually, **but** the government does not attempt to restrict their numbers.
3 Tourists can import dangerous diseases into a country. In addition to **this**, they can smuggle illegal items into a country.

4 People who don't travel often have preconceived ideas about other countries and cultures. **In contrast**, people who do travel often have a more realistic idea and don't make generalisations about other countries.

5 Even though tourists are often asked to cover their shoulders when visiting religious buildings, they often ignore this request.

6 Besides releasing greenhouse gases, aeroplanes also create noise pollution.

7 Tourists often want to stay in remote places. **However**, they often complain when they find they can't get a wifi signal.

8 Tourists should consider 'green holidays' in order to protect the environment. **What is more**, they should consider train travel as an alternative to flying.

4   Sample answer

These days, it is possible for professionals and tourists to travel to areas which have been inaccessible until now, such as the South Pole, deserts and mountain ranges. This increased accessibility has both benefits and drawbacks, which this essay will discuss.

For professionals interested in finding out about our environment, the possibility of visiting remote places can only be a good thing. Based on their visits and research carried out there, scientists can draw conclusions about the state of the environment, which will be used to make decisions which have the potential to benefit us all. For example, by monitoring the rate that the polar icecaps are melting, scientists can estimate the severity of global warming and advise governments about cutting back on emissions.

With regard tourists, however, the benefits and drawbacks are more mixed. On the one hand, if tourists visit a remote place and use their visit to learn more about the natural environment, this could raise their awareness of the need to cherish and protect similar places and the species that live there. On the other hand, not all tourists are responsible and their presence could disturb or even damage the wildlife in remote places. In addition, tourists require facilities, which can often lead to decisions to cut down trees and to build construct shops, cafes and tourist centres, thereby damaging the natural environment. This, along with water pollution and littering, is what has happened in certain mountainous areas of Nepal, which have become popular with tourists.

In conclusion, whilst the accessibility of remote places to scientists generally brings benefits, the results of tourists gaining access to places that are 'off the beaten track' are more mixed.

Rocks on the move (pages 26–27)

1   Students' own answers.

2a   transport, deposit, form, melt, weather, metamorphose

2b   1 transports 2 deposited 3 melted

2c   Students' own answers.

3a   Suggested answer: probably with weathering, as it's the start of the rock's journey. Alternatively, a candidate could start with the formation of rocks deep underground over thousands of years.

3b   Students' own answers.

3c   1a

4a   **1** Rocks are transported (by rivers) down mountain sides and deposited into the ocean, where they sink to the bottom as sediment.
2 The eroded rock is squeezed together by the weight of the water and other materials, in order to form sedimentary rock.
3 Sedimentary rock is changed to metamorphic rock by heat and pressure, via volcanic activity.
4 no change – doesn't need to be put into the passive: metamorphic rock either gradually works its way up to the earth's surface, or it melts to form magma.
5 no change – doesn't need to be put into the passive: The magma then cools underground or erupts and * cools on the Earth's surface, where the elements and other forces begin the weathering process.

4b   Students' own answers.

4c   **1** eventually. **3** At times **4** At other times **5** once again

5a   Students' own answers.

5b   **Sample answer**

The diagram shows the way that the element nitrogen circulates around our natural environment.

We can see from the diagram that 79% of the earth's atmosphere consists of nitrogen gas. However, in order for nitrogen to be moved to the earth's surface, it needs to be converted by lightning which enables it to combine with oxygen. It then falls to earth through the process of precipitation.

Once there, nitrogen can be broken down by bacteria and fungi which enable it to become nitrogen compound and eventually allow it to be assimilated and used by plants. Animals consume these plants and nitrogen is returned to the soil via animal dung. Some of the nitrogen compounds are made into nitrogen gas by the bacteria underground and once again released into the atmosphere.

Overall, we can see that the nitrogen cycle is entirely natural and nitrogen is moved around the environment by a number of different processes.

Doing damage (pages 28–29)

1a **a)** urban overpopulation
b) waste
c) air pollution
d) waste, urban overpopulation
e) air pollution
f) air pollution
g) waste, urban overpopulation
h) encourage people to over-exploit natural resources
i) waste
j) air pollution
k) urban overpopulation
l) waste
m) urban overpopulation
n) air pollution
o) waste

1b Students' own answers.

2a **1** Just a few. Suggest a maximum of three problems
2 This is subjective, but probably four: introduction, outline of problems, outline of solutions, conclusion
3 The balance can be equal, but it's probably more important to dedicate more space and time to the solutions.

2b Students' own answers.

3 Play a part
Make an effort
Have a viable alternative
Impose higher taxes
Improve the infrastructure
Take responsibility
Avoid buying foodstuffs
Tackle the problems
Decrease harm
Take steps
Suggest measures
Address issues

4a Impose higher taxes
Improve public transport infrastructure
To have a viable alternative

4b **a)** If we don't, it is likely that before very soon, our world will not be inhabitable.
b) If driving became too expensive and people had a viable alternative, they would opt for public transport.
c) If we don't, it is likely that before very soon, our world will not be inhabitable.
d) If driving became too expensive and people had a viable alternative, they would opt for public transport.

5 Students' own answers.

6a No, just solutions

6b **Sample answer**
Urban sprawl caused by increasing populations mean that many countries are losing their areas of rural beauty. There are a number of advantages to protecting these areas, which this essay will outline. It will also suggest steps that can be taken to prevent beauty spots being lost.

Protecting areas such as parks, forests and coast line has benefits for the environment. Without trees and plants, there would be nothing to absorb carbon dioxide from our atmosphere and we would also lose important producers of oxygen. Natural areas also absorb surface water which runs off the concrete in urban areas, thereby preventing flooding.

Preserving rural areas is also of direct benefit to humans. There have been a number of studies that have found that our sense of well-being is heightened by spending time in nature and our levels of stress are decreased. With many people living in stressful city environments, green spaces are more necessary than ever.

One way of preventing beauty spots from being damaged is for the government to put preservation orders on them. For instance, they can turn them into areas of 'outstanding natural beauty'. This recognition prevents developers from building on beauty spots. Another way of protecting natural areas is to involve the public in their maintenance. Volunteers can plant trees and patrol areas. They can also help to create footpaths through these areas in order to increase the public's appreciation and understanding of natural beauty.

In conclusion, there are a number of benefits to preserving natural areas; these are both environmental and social. These areas can be most effectively preserved by the government introducing preservation orders.

All the right gear (pages 30–31)

1a aerobics: lycra leggings or jogging pants, or shorts, gym or aerobics room basketball: shorts and a T-shirt, court, ball, nets; football:
football kit, pitch, ball,
goals; golf: golf shoes, trousers / skirt and top, course, clubs and balls;
skateboarding: boarding clothes, a helmet, a skateboard, a skateboard park or
slope; tennis: tennis whites, court, net, racquet, balls

1b Students' own answers

2a Students' own answers.

2b in order to, so as to, so that …

2c **1** glue **2** reinforce **3** assemble **4** sew **5** mould **6** insert **7** reduce

2d **1** First of all, pieces of leather comprising the top part of the shoe are cut out of a large piece of leather.
2 Next, the pieces of leather around the toe and heel of the trainer known as the toe cap and heel counter are reinforced with plastic.

3a Students should, where possible, use verbs which are not included in the diagram, in order to show range of vocabulary. They could also convert nouns in the diagram into verbs where appropriate. Suggestions: apply, combine, stack, drill, bolt, smooth, seal, decorate, join.

3b **Sample answer**

The diagram shows the manufacturing process of the wooden deck of a skateboard.

First of all, glue is applied with a glue machine to the layers of maple wood veneer which will eventually be combined to make the deck.

After that, seven pieces of maple wood veneer are stacked together and put under considerable pressure using a mechanical mold, which gives a skateboard its distinctive curved shape. Following this stage, holes are drilled into either end of the deck using a device called a 'drilling rig'. These holes are to enable the wheels and their frame to be bolted onto the deck after it is completed.

The deck is then sanded so as to make it smooth and then sealed so that it is waterproof and can be cleaned easily. Finally, using a screen printing technique, the deck is decorated with its own unique design.

The deck is then ready to be joined with the skateboard wheels and frame before being packaged and shipped to suppliers.

The dangers of technology (pages 32–33)

1a Students' own answers.
1b Students' own answers.
1c Students' own answers.

2a Students' own answers.
2b **a)** 3 **b)** 4 **c)** 1 **d)** 2
2c **1** c) **2** a) **3** d) **4** b)
2d **1** commit **2** psychological **3** financial **4** restrict **5** establish **6** summarize **7** communicative

3a Students' own answers.
3b **Sample answer**

Research has found that while playing games on the computer has some benefits, it also has a number of potentially damaging effects on children. This essay will examine the nature of these drawbacks and suggest ways of tackling them.

A number of papers have been written which cite playing violent computer games as the cause of increased aggressive thoughts in children. The interactive nature of violent computer games is damaging as children are rewarded for carrying out violent actions such as killing, stabbing and shooting their 'enemies' repeatedly. What is more, there is no indication that such actions are morally wrong or that there are peaceful alternatives to violence. This can

lead to children who do not view negotiation as an option.

Non-violent computer games have their own negative effects. If children play them for hours on end, this can have a detrimental impact on their school work and decrease the time that children spend socialising and developing their interpersonal skills. Group gaming can also encourage online bullying as children can be prevented from joining a particular group.

There are steps that parents can take to prevent these negative effects damaging their children's well-being. For example, they can situate a child's computer in a place that will allow them to monitor the games. In addition, parents can supervise the acquisition of games and pay attention to the parental guidance labels. Thirdly, parents can negotiate time that children spend gaming. Above all, though, parents need to educate children about the dangers of excessive gaming.

In conclusion, there are a number of dangers associated with computer games that parents need to mitigate. One of the most important things that they can do is educate their children about the dangers involved and how to avoid them.

Going green (pages 34–35)

1 Students' own answers.

2 Students' own answers.

3 **1** actor **2** lights **3** natural **4** backlight **5** fill light **6** shadow

4a **1** system **2** enables **3** allows **4** so as to **5** in order to **6** consists **7** prevents
4b Students' own answers.
4c Students' own answers.

5a 2 Key parts involved in the piano's action
3 Stages of action
1 Summary of what the diagram shows

5b **Sample answer**

The diagram shows the inside workings of a grand piano and demonstrates how a note on a piano is created.

The piano is a musical instrument that consists of a large wooden outside casing, a keyboard, pedals, a lid which can be opened and a number of internal moving parts. These parts comprise of a hammer, a damper and a string.

The note starts when the pianist pushes one of the black or white keys on the keyboard. If the pianist also presses down on the piano's pedals, the note can be made longer or softer. In addition, opening the lid of the piano will enable the pianist to make the notes louder.

When the keys are pressed down, a hammer hits a string in the piano, which causes it to vibrate and to produce a noise. The damper prevents the note from continuing for too long because it touches the string to cease the vibration as soon as the key is released.

Artistic licence (pages 36–37)

1a   Students' own answers.
1b   Students' own answers.

2   A

3a   negative
3b

Word	Type of information it refers to	Example from essay
it	a 'dummy' pronoun used when the sentence does not have a subject. Often used with phrases such as It is a fact that …/ It is widely believed that …	**1** It is now common-place to look at art online.
it	refers backwards or forwards to a noun phrase or an idea	Arguably, the virtual existence of an artwork also makes **5** it more commonplace.
its	The possessive of a pronoun	**6** This could lead to people ceasing to appreciate **7** its details and value.
this	refers backwards or forwards to a phrase or idea	**6** This could lead to people ceasing to appreciate **7** its details and value.
which	a relative pronoun which replaces the object of the previous clause	**3** This inevitably results in fewer visits to art galleries, **4** which decreases the income of art institutions
one	Refers backwards or forwards to a singular noun	**C** Galleries have tried to keep up with the popularity of technology by including information about **8** their collections on their websites and by giving visitors the opportunity to have the virtual experience of an artwork alongside the real **9** one.
their	The possessive plural pronoun	**C** Galleries have tried to keep up with the popularity of technology by including information about **8** their collections on their websites and by giving visitors the opportunity to have the virtual experience of an artwork alongside the real **9** one.

3c   **10** which **11** it **12** it **13** this **14** it **15** it **16** it

4a   … On the other hand, illegal downloads can have a positive effect on the artist. The artist can find new and innovative ways of selling their music. For example, it is possible to release a digital album for free as well as one at a higher price. This album would have exclusive content and personal details /which has exclusive content and personal details at a higher price that / which fans would be prepared to pay for. New bands can also offer a single from a new album to download. Making it available often encourages fans to buy the whole album and to spread the word about it on social media. This increases its likelihood of selling well when the album is released.

4b   **Sample answer**
While the internet has made it easier for musicians to reach their audience, it has also made it far easier for the public to download music free of charge or at a cost far below the recommended retail price for a record. This essay explores the effects that this has on the musician, both positive and negative.

On one hand, it is obvious that illegal downloads will have a negative impact on the musician's record sales. It has been reported that music sales in the US alone have dropped by around 50% since 1999. As record companies have seen their profits decrease, they have had to make people in their teams redundant. This includes sound engineers, producers and technicians. What is more, declining profits and fewer staff mean that there is less scope for record companies to invest in new talents, leading to a potential stagnation of the music industry.

On the other hand, illegal downloads can have a positive effect on the artist. The artist can find new and innovative ways of selling their music. For example, it is possible to release a digital album for free as well as one which has exclusive content and personal details at a higher price that / which fans would be prepared to pay for. New bands can also offer a single from a new album to download. Making it available often encourages fans to buy the whole album and to spread the word about it on social media. This increases its likelihood of selling well when it is released.

To conclude, there is ample evidence to suggest that that the music industry is suffering because of illegal downloading and peer-to-peer file sharing. However, for musicians who are prepared to think outside the box, it is still possible to make a profit.

Mechanical motion (pages 38–39)

1a
1 h sailing ship: late 1500s
2 j submarine: 1620
3 e horse-drawn bus: 1662
4 f hot air balloon: 1783
5 l steam-powered locomotive: 1804
6 d glider: 1853
7 g motorcycle: 1867
8 c car: 1883 (powered by an internal combustion engine
9 b airship: 1900
10 a aeroplane: 1903

1b Students' own answers.

2a Students' own answers.
2b A It became smaller

3a
1 were introduced; appeared
2 propelled, powered by
3 antecedents, predecessor, earlier models

3b
larger
lighter
taller
further
more comfortable
more easily and quickly

3c
around
quite
far
considerably
much

4 **Sample answer**

The diagram shows the progression of a bus' design in the 19th and 20th centuries.

Over time the bus remained roughly rectangular in shape. However its size increased and it also became more efficient to run.

The earliest bus, known as the horse bus, consisted of a single deck and was made to carry approximately 20 people. The speed that the horse could pull it was limited by its narrow wheels. After this, in 1853, the horse-drawn omnibus appeared, which had a higher capacity than its predecessor due to the addition of an upper deck.
At the end of the nineteenth century, electricity replaced the horse and the trolley bus was invented, followed by the motor bus in 1897. This last invention resembled the buses of today, but it had an engine at the front and an entrance at the rear. A conductor was employed at the rear to check tickets. In the 1960s,

the diesel powered bus became popular. This was more powerful than the petrol bus and had an entrance at the front to enable the driver to check tickets. This bus also had a higher capacity than any of the former buses, seating up to 72 people.

Global gridlock (pages 40–41)

1a Students' own answers.
1b Students' own answers.

2a 1 an opinion essay A 2 C 3 B
2b A
2c Overall, the writer disagrees with the statement in the question
2d
1 Rephrases the main question being answered
2 Summarises the main points of the essay.
3 Clearly states your own position.
4 Introduce new material …

3 It is undeniable that there are many arguments in favour of an increased use of public transport. A greater number of buses and a higher frequency of trains would result in fewer cars on the roads and therefore less pollution. However, what is needed is a practical, feasible solution to the traffic congestion problem.
Unfortunately, many existing public transport systems offer a poor service and the vehicles are old and not environmentally friendly. Only by replacing them with a completely new system would the environment benefit substantially and this would be economically unfeasible, especially during our current financial crisis. It would also take an impractically long time to overhaul public transport systems. On balance, then, I believe that encouraging commuters to use public transport rather than cars is not the best solution. Instead, it is a better idea to reduce traffic on the roads by introducing a congestion charge.

4a **Sample plan**
Increasing the price of petrol is the best way to solve growing traffic and pollution problems. To what extent do you agree or disagree? What other measures do you think might be effective?

Agree	Disagree
It will discourage drivers from making non-essential journeys	If no other form of transport is available, drivers have to use cars and have no other choice but to pay higher prices.
It may encourage families to own just one car.	It's immoral – benefits the oil companies and government rather than the environment.
Other measures?	
Car sharing, alternative sources of fuel (biofuel) or electricity	

4b   Sample conclusion
To conclude, while putting up the price of fuel may discourage some drivers from making non-essential journeys and encourage some families to rely on just one car, it is not likely to make a big enough difference to have a positive effect on the environment, as drivers are still likely to use their cars. The move will also benefit government above all. It is, this essay argues, better to invest in research into alternative sources of fuel, which would be a more sustainable and far-reaching solution.

Sweet tooth (pages 42–43)

1   5 teaspoons; Students' own answers.

2a   4
2b   Students' own answers.
2c   The bar graph illustrates the <u>amount of sugar</u> people between the ages of one and a half and 65 years of age <u>consumed</u> over four years as a percentage of their total energy intake, <u>in comparison to</u> the recommended maximum energy percentage. The two pie charts <u>break</u> the sugar consumption of three of the age groups included in the graph <u>into</u> different food groups.
2d   **1** A Both males and females of 11-18 years took in the highest amounts of sugar, at 16 and 15.2 percent of their food energy respectively B 4 to 18 year olds who ate the most sugar did so in the form of soft drinks, and biscuits, cakes and puddings; these two food groups contributed 45 and 30 percent. In contrast adults of 19 to 64 years consumed far more table sugar, at 17% as opposed to around 7% in the younger age groups.
2 There probably isn't the space to mention children of 1.5-3 years in the graph, especially because this age range isn't covered in the pie charts. There is also not really the necessity to mention the food groups in the pie charts other than those which are the smallest and biggest contributors to sugar intake at the different ages.
3 Students' own answers, but suggest that starting with the graph makes more sense because it gives a more general picture of all age ranges.

3a   Students' own answers.
3b   **1** Respectively enables candidates to avoid repeating 'males / females of 11-18'. Did so, allows candidates to avoid repeating 'ate the most sugar.'
2 as males and females of 11-18.

4   Sample answer
The table compares the number of food advertisements, categorised by product type, viewed by teenagers in 2012 and the graph charts the number of advertisements viewed by a variety of age groups, including teenagers between 2009 and 2012. The graph shows us that between 2009 and 2012,

teenagers viewed fewer advertisements than adults of 18-49 years, but considerably more than children between 2 and 5 years, and 6 and 11 years, who were exposed to around 1,000 and 1,250 respectively every year.
We can also see that with three of the age groups (12–17, 18–24 and 25–49) the number of adverts viewed dropped steadily between 2009 and 2011 but then rose to around the original figure in 2012. The table breaks down the type of adverts that teenagers watched during the peak viewing year of 2012. We can see that by far the highest number of adverts viewed were for food consumed at lunch and dinner, followed by those for convenience and value food and then by kids' meals, at 119.6 advertisements. Significantly, far more of this last category of advert were targeted at teenagers than adults.

Modern maladies (pages 44–45)

1   **a)** the number of cases of diabetes is rising **b)** diabetes occurs because of excess body weight and lack of physical activity

2a   Students' own answers
2b   1 2 **2** 1 **3** 3

3   2 is probably more successful as it explains the opening statement by giving examples. It also uses a greater quantity of synonyms to avoid repeating words in the question.

4a   **1** Suggested answer: probably four including introduction and conclusion.
2 1: introduction, paragraph **2**: how lifestyles have effected our diet; **3**: whether candidate feels that these developments are positive or negative; **4** conclusion
4b   Students' own answers
5a   An overwhelmingly negative development
5b   Has led to … becoming
Mean less sleep
Long days increase the likelihood of our relaxing..
This results in
Poor diet will cause many people to
Sufferers can also develop kidney failure
… heart attacks as a result of the disease
Moving less is likely to have a highly detrimental effect …
5c   **1** lead to **2** means **3** increases the likelihood **4** this results in **5** can also develop **6** trigger

6   Sample answer
In recent years, there has been a growth in population due to life expectancy in the elderly increasing in a number of countries. This essay will evaluate whether this is a positive or negative development.

On a personal level, many members of the population benefit from the increase in life expectancy. Retired people have more time to enjoy themselves and are likely to be healthy enough to enjoy holidays abroad and to take up new hobbies and perhaps even to become mature students. Their families also benefit from their good health because grandparents may be willing and able to care for their grandchildren, who will benefit from their life experience and the close bond that they share.

On a financial level, however, increased life expectancy results in the government needing to budget for far bigger pension funds and also leads to more money being spent on the provision of care for the elderly. It also means that a greater strain is put onto health care systems when care homes cannot cope with meeting the elderly's medical needs. A bigger elderly population also leads to housing issues. Older people may choose to stay in their family homes for the duration of their lives, meaning that there are fewer homes available for younger families.

Overall, I believe that the benefits of increased life expectancy outweigh the disadvantages. Families benefit from the presence of older people and having more time allows pensioners some well-deserved relaxation after working and contributing to the economy for the majority of their lives.

A change of plan (pages 46–47)

1 Students' own answers.

2a The proposed development of a shopping complex. The candidate would use present and future tenses.

2b/2c **1** The first picture shows the current layout of a shopping complex, and the second shows some planned changes to its space and purpose.
2 It is clear that significant changes will be made in terms of the number, type and size of shops and to the delivery and parking space. Two shops will be **5** replaced by one and the parking space will be **6** reduced.
3 The footprint of the existing stores will also be **7** enlarged (enlargement), to occupy space currently **8** dedicated (dedication) to the lorry park. This will mean parking space will be **9** halved (half). Inside the supermarket, an open plan space will be **10** divided(division) by aisles and checkouts will be **11** situated (situation) near to the new entrance.
4 At present, a Chinese food store and newsagents **1** occupy (occupation) the north East corner of the complex. However the plan is to **2** combine (combination) the floor space of both stores, by **3** demolishing(demolition) the dividing wall and **4** replacing (replacement) the existing stores with a German supermarket.

2d They are different: they are not parallel.

3 **1** The entrance has been expanded to avoid trolleys getting stuck and <u>to avoid queues of people at the</u> entrance at busy times: people queuing at the entrance at busy times.
2 Not only has the staircase been demolished <u>and the door has been moved too</u>; but the door has been moved.
3 Neither the function of the gallery <u>or its basic floorplan has changed</u>; nor its basic floorplan has changed
4 The disadvantages of having an open plan space is overcrowding in particular areas and <u>the passengers become confused about the direction they should move in</u>: confusion about the direction passengers should move in..

4 Students' own answers.

5 **Sample answer**
The diagrams show changes that were made to an airport departure lounge between the years 2010 and 2016.

Overall, we can see that a great many more shops and restaurants were constructed and the passenger experience was more carefully controlled in terms of the path they took through the lounge.

In 2010, the departure lounge was an open plan area, which allowed passengers to roam freely and move in different directions in order to visit the shops around the outside of the lounge. There were seats in the centre of the lounge surrounding a small bar, which could have become crowded, as there was only one other café in the lounge.

Although there were still seats available in 2015, they could only be reached by passengers travelling down a number of designated walkways to reach them. This meant that the number of passengers occupying seats were likely to be fewer, as some other passengers may have opted for different walkways, that took them past cafes and restaurants, or past shops. In addition, the new layout of the lounge was more space efficient so that more shops and restaurants could be accommodated.

The walkways meant that passengers were all likely to be walking in the same direction, causing less chaos than in 2010.

Global village (pages 48–49)

1 Students' own answers.

2a Students' own answers.

2b It has been said that the world has become a 'global village'; a place in which / where people of all nationalities can communicate and trade without being limited by their country of origin. There are many advantages to this development and some disadvantages. This essay will examine both.

To examine the benefits first, business is becoming increasingly international and globalisation allows for everyone to communicate easily using a lingua franca: English. Our modes of communication are also globalized; email, phone and texts, they are not limited by borders and facilitate quick communication. The exchange of goods and services around he world means that people living in countries with limited resources can access goods which / that can significantly improve their quality of life. Globalisation also encourages multi-nationals to invest in the workforce in developing countries, thereby creating employment in these countries. Trade between nations develops political understanding because countries benefit from one another's assets and forge trade agreements.

3a Paragraph B is easier to read because it is more cohesive.

It contains linking words and phrases and pronouns that refer backwards and forwards to nouns in the text.

It also repeats nouns and uses synonyms of key nouns.

B On the other hand, there are some disadvantages to globalisation, for example, unemployment. International businesses tend to move their businesses to a country where labour is cheap, and this move often necessitates making existing employees redundant. When new employees in developing countries are taken on, it is sometimes at a very low wage and a new employee does not always enjoy very favourable working conditions. A further negative impact of globalisation is that it can affect the environment. With globalization, people no longer buy and eat locally grown food or other products; they often consume goods which have been developed and grown abroad. Transporting these products has led to an increase in pollution levels. The increase in production of food and crops which results from an increase in consumption due to globalisation also leads to a greater amount of industrial waste being produced and having to be disposed of.

3b B On the other hand, there are some disadvantages to globalisation, for example, unemployment. International businesses tend to move their businesses to a country where labour is cheap, and <u>this move</u> often necessitates making <u>existing employees</u> redundant. When <u>new employees</u> in developing countries are taken on, it is sometimes at a very low wage and <u>a new employee</u> does not always enjoy very favourable working conditions. <u>A further negative impact of globalisation</u> is that it can affect the environment. <u>With globalization</u>, people no longer buy and eat locally grown food or other products; they often consume goods which have been developed and grown abroad. Transporting <u>these</u> products has led to an increase in pollution levels. The increase in production of food and crops <u>which results from an increase in</u>

<u>consumption due to globalisation</u> also leads to a greater amount of industrial waste being produced and having to be disposed of.

3c **1** whilst **2** it **3** these **4** However **5** it **6** globalisation **7** its

4a **Sample answer**

Some people complain that whichever city in the world they visit, they see the same brands advertised and the same shops. Whilst this does have its disadvantages, there are a number of advantages to globalisation that this essay will outline.

Admittedly, cultural homogeneity has its drawbacks. When one dominant culture is preferred, this often leads to other cultures, often those native to a particular country, becoming less popular and therefore to traditions dying out. An example of this is clothing. If people of a country prefer to wear clothes from the US, for instance, they may abandon their own national costume in order to do so. What is more, globalisation sometimes encourages people to make unhealthy choices; the worldwide spread of fast food outlets is not necessarily a positive development.

However, I would argue that this is a small price to pay for the opportunities that globalisation affords. It is surely a mark of progress that people in some countries are not restricted to a single culture, but are able to choose to adopt fashions and brands from different cultures. Globalisation also brings with it an understanding and appreciation of people from other countries. If, for instance, different populations watch the same TV programme, we understand that we all share a similar sense of humour, for example.

In summary, it is my view that the advantages of globalisation far outweigh the disadvantages. Whilst it doesn't prevent people from keeping to their own cultural traditions, it does offer them options and encourages them to appreciate other cultures.

4b Students' own answers

Caught on camera (pages 50–51)

1a Students' own answers

1b According to the text, the purpose of CCTV cameras is to cut crime and increase public security. The text concludes that there are both advantages and disadvantages to CCTV.

2a **1** Students' own answers. Suggested answer: vandalism, theft.
2 Overall, we can see that as the number of car parks with live CCTV cameras increased the nmber of recorded crimes decreased.

2b That CCTV cameras seem to be an effective deterrent against crimes being committed.

3a Articles are missing. The teacher has <u>underlined</u> mistakes with articles and plurals.

3b/3c The line graph illustrates the number of crimes that were committed in ~~the~~ car parks over *a* four year period, both a year before and three years after the introduction of ~~the~~ live CCTV cameras.

Overall, it can be seen that, as *the* number of CCTV cameras installed increased, *the* number of crimes committed decreased, although there <u>were</u> sharp rises and falls in ~~the~~ crime numbers throughout each year.

Looking at the graph in more detail, *the* number of crimes peaked in July 2000, when just under 140 committed. This number then fell sharply to *a* low of 30 the following year, only to <u>picked</u> up again to approximately 90 crimes in July 2001, which was when the first CCTV camera was installed.

Shortly after that, in July 2002, when there were 20 CCTV <u>cameras</u>, *the* number of crimes had fallen to 60. Thereafter, when *the* number of cameras was almost <u>tripled</u> to 58 in January 2003, the crime rate dipped to zero. Although it did rise sharply to 40 crimes over *the* next few months, it continued to be low and didn't surpass 10 crimes for *the* remainder of 2003.

4 Sample answer

The table shows the impact that CCTV systems had on the number of recorded crimes committed between 2016 and 2018 in a number of areas.

Overall, it can be observed that the installation of CCTV cameras resulted in fewer crimes being committed in the areas featured in the table.

The area where the drop in crime was highest was in car parks, where the crime rate decreased by 73%. Although the crime rate was highest in the area of Cambrook, it only fell by 10% over the two years specified. The crime rate in the city suburbs was second highest but the drop after cameras were installed was larger than in Cambrook, at 28%

There were two areas in which the crime rate actually rose following the installation of cameras. The area where the rise was most significant was in Markham, where crime increased by 18%. In contrast, the rise in the council estate was relatively small; just .3 of a percent.

Causes of crime (pages 52–53)

1a **1** c; e **2** b **3** a **4** d; f; g
1b Students' own answers

2a Problem–solution
2b Students' own answers
2c **2** unhappy childhood; education
4 criminals; bad influence; job
5 vocational training
6 community service
7 accommodation; work

3a **a)** 1 **b)** 9 **c)** 4 **d)** 5 **e)** 2 **f)** 3 **g)** 7 **h)** 8 **i)** 10 **j)** 6

It is a commonly known fact that a prison sentence does not necessarily reform a criminal. This essay will explore the reasons for this and suggest steps that could be taken to avoid criminals re-offending. Criminals often turn to crime because they feel that they have no other choice. They are often had **1** <u>an unhappy childhood</u> and are sometimes deprived of the opportunity to gain qualifications and therefore to earn money legally. Once a criminal is serving a **4** <u>custodial sentence</u>, they will inevitably come into contact with other criminals, many of whom can **5** <u>be a negative influence</u>. Even if a prisoner wants to **6** <u>live a crime free life</u>, it is difficult to do so as a **7** <u>criminal record</u> makes it challenging to find a job.

There are, however, ways that the criminal justice system can help criminals **8** <u>avoid the vicious circle of reoffending</u>. For instance, they can provide the prisoner with vocational training, so that an inmate can enter into **9** <u>suitable trades on release.</u> Another way of reducing the number of **10** <u>repeat offenders</u> is to avoid sending them to prison at all. Community service will underline **11** <u>a community's value</u> to a criminal and dissuade them from damaging it further.

In conclusion, despite the fact that there are many understandable reasons why criminals continue to follow a life of crime, there are **12** <u>many solutions to this situation</u>, ranging from equipping prisoners with useful life skills, to encouraging them to help in the community.

3b **1** a, e, h **2** g, j, i **3** b, c, d, f
3c Students' own answers.

4 Sample answer

It is undeniable that crime amongst adolescents has increased and many people blame the increase in violence in films and TV programmes. In this essay, I explain why I agree that the media one of the main causes in the rise in juvenile crime. I will also suggest ways that society can address this issue.

Adolescents are highly susceptible human beings. They have reached an age where they are trying to find their own path in life. It is natural that they look for role models in the media, as they tend to spend a large proportion of their time in front of a screen. Fit, attractive film starts are compelling role models, but unfortunately, these characters often lack moral fibre and commit violent acts without suffering any consequences. This can lead adolescents to believe that violence is an easy solution to issues in their lives and that it is somehow 'cool' to act in this way.

Whilst it is tempting to view young adults as independent people capable of making their own decisions, we must remember that they lack life experience and are vulnerable. It makes sense therefore, for parents to protect teenagers from negative influences to a degree, by monitoring TV programmes and films that they are exposed to.

It is also a good idea for parents and teenagers to introduce teenagers to more positive role models, who may not be as high profile as those in the media, but who could have a positive influence on teenagers.

Overall, although I am convinced that the media plays a large part in encouraging violent behaviour in young adults, I believe that there are, without doubt, steps that we can take to combat this issue, ranging from protecting teenagers from unsuitable violence to exposing them to more positive role models.

Social trends (pages 54–55)

1a 1 Students' own answers. 2 Students' own answers.

1b Students' own answers; Present tense

2a 15–25 year olds

2b They've repeated the words in the graph.
The bar graph illustrates the percentage of adults who visited social networking sites in the UK over a seven year period. The data is broken down by sex and by age group.

2c 1 increased 2 was 3 used 4 followed 5 spent 6 reached 7 was 8 was not 9 rose 10 was not 11 rose 12 saw

3a Two: present perfect, future forms (Although if the candidate gave figures from specific years in the past, they would need to use the past simple.)

3b 1 has been 2 was 3 is predicted; is thought to be likely 4 It is probable; will continue /

4 **Sample answer**

The graph shows the amount of income that has been generated by digital advertising in the US between 2015 and 2018 and the income that is likely to be generated between 2018 and 2021.

Overall, we can observe that the biggest income generator over the whole period is internet search. We can also see that between 2015 and 2018, revenue from all five advertising types has increased, with the biggest increase in the income generated by social media.

In the future this increase looks set to continue, with internet search revenue increasing by around two thousand dollars year on year. Other types of advertising are expected to have slightly slower rates of growth. The revenue from social media is predicted to rise by around one thousand dollars per year. The same is likely to apply to video and social media. The advertisement type that has generated the smallest revenue since 2015 is likely only to increase it's revenue by around 150 dollars each year until 2021.

Spreading the news (pages 56–57)

1 1 Students' own answer. 2 Students' own answer. 3 Students' own answer. 4 d 5 1a stories about a particular event b regular news items throughout the day c a news item which is broadcast because of an event which has just happened
2a a copy of a newspaper b where the newspaper is old and read c people who read the newspaper

2a Not really, because the essay question uses a superlative – the most important – which means that the candidate must reply to this. However, the candidate can offer other options.

2b In the second paragraph, the writer explains why newspapers won't be the only source of news. In the third paragraph, the writer explains why internet based news is more relevant, but also suggests reasons
why it is unlikely to entirely replace print newspapers.

2c/2d A 5 the older generation, who are used to…
B 4 internet based; frequently updated
C 1 having read a story
D 3 due to it being easier
E 2 the readership of online newspapers who are currently enjoying

3a The writer agrees

3b 1 preventing 2 an independent and well-informed opinion 3 a distorted view 4 worthy of being featured 5 leaving the reader ignorant 6 happening around the world 7 Having outlined 8 Choosing / a person choosing

3c **Sample answer**
It is an undeniable fact that newspapers shape people's feelings on current affairs. Unfortunately, they often abuse their power to do so by publishing sensationalist stories. This essay argues that whilst their influence can be negative, they are also an important source of information.

The primary aim of newspapers is to sell news. This often means that stories are published with attention-grabbing headlines and the most lurid stories are printed on the front page. This can mean that readers miss out on more newsworthy stories. Readers' understanding of world events may also be imbalanced because tabloid newspaper reporters might write a story which substantiates a particular fear felt by their readership. These stories may seem evidence-based, but are often unreliable. Unfortunately, they may fuel the fears of readers, which can lead readers to make prejudiced decisions.

That said, whilst both tabloid and broadsheet newspapers tend to 'frame' stories so that they align with their chosen political perspective, it is perhaps better for the public to have access to some news than none at all. Complete ignorance would mean a very badly informed public, who would make decisions based purely on gut instinct. What is more, newspaper stories, particularly broadsheet ones, are generally based on fact. It could be argued that it's the reader's responsibility to choose their newspaper carefully and to keep in mind that stories always represent someone's unique perspective on an issue.

To sum up, newspaper journalists are motivated to sell newspapers. This, together with the bias of individual papers means that the news readers get is seldom disinterested or balanced. However, an educated reader is preferable to one that takes no interest in current affairs. This essay has argued that it is the responsibility of the reader to select the news he or she reads judiciously.

Practice test: Task 1

Sample answer: Band 7 score

The carbon cycle is the process by which carbon moves from the atmosphere into the Earth and its organisms and then back again.

Plants take in carbon dioxide, which is a form of carbon, from the atmosphere to make carbohydrates through photosynthesis. Animals feed on the plant, therefore carbon compounds are passed along the food chain. Most of the carbon animals consumed is then exhaled as carbon dioxide through the process of respiration. The animals and plants will die eventually. They are eaten by decomposers and the carbon in their bodies is returned into the atmosphere. The decomposed plants and animals are formed as fossil fuels over millions of years. These fossil fuels are then burnt as a source of energy, and carbon dioxide is given off through this process. In this way, carbon compounds are released into the atmosphere and the cycle repeats as carbon moves through many organisms again.

Examiner commentary

This task 1 answer is of an appropriate length (151 words). A clear overview of the main stages of the process is presented and the information is logically organised. Cohesive devices are used appropriately but are limited in range. A good range of lexis is used and some complex structures such as relative clauses are used in error-free sentences. There are a few inappropriate examples of word choice (they are eaten by decomposers).

Sample answer: Band 6 score

Carbon is used repeatedly in a process called the carbon cycle. Plants take in carbon dioxide in air. Animals absorb carbon dioxide by eating the plants and then they breathe to release the carbon dioxide. The plants and animals eventually die. The carbon in their bodies will returned to the atmosphere. Over millions of years, fossil fuels such as coal, oil and nature gas can be formed. Afterwards, people burn fossil fuels and use it as a kind of energy.

Examiner commentary

This task 1 answer received a lower band score because it lacked detail and was too short (81 words). However, it does contain a short overview and the information and ideas are arranged coherently. Cohesive devices are used effectively and there is an adequate range of vocabulary for the task. There are very few errors in spelling or word formation. Sentences are mostly simple, but there is one example of a complex sentence (Animals absorb carbon dioxide by eating the plants and then they breathe to release the carbon dioxide.)

Practice test: Task 2

Sample answer: Band 6 score

Whether to send a child to a co-ed or single sex school is a matter which is hotly debated and has been for a long time. Some people think that mixed schools have benefits for both boys and girls, whilst some disagree, claiming that boys and girls learn differently and students are better taught separately.

Majority of parents believe that going to a single sex school can result in better grades, which is true, supported by difference in academic results between two types of schools, because boy and girls learn differently; a research has pointed out that boys concentrate better in a cold room whilst girls focus better in a warm environment. This means that teaching method and environment have to be more tailored to suit the gender of the student. In addition, in a single sex environment, girls or boys are not be ashamed to break traditional ideas of gender- orientated decisions, for instance, girls can do physics and mathematics, while boys can do textiles and art.

However, I have an opposite thought to the above. If they are in a mixed school, they will be offered a wider range of opportunities. If they are in a mixed school, they can have access to resources in unpopular fields in their gender. Students should also be exposed to the reality, where both sexes exist, otherwise later social problem can be seen.

In conclusion, there are benefits to both single sex schools and co-ed schools. For example, in a single sex environment, lessons can be adjusted to fit one sex, and students are more encouraged to try subjects in different fields. But, in a mixed school, students are able to figure out their talents in different areas, and develop their social skills.

Examiner commentary

The candidate addresses all parts of the task, though the advantages of a mixed sex school are underdeveloped. In general, the information and ideas are arranged coherently. There are parts of the essay where cohesion between sentences is faulty (Majority of parents believe that going to a single sex school can result in better grades, which is true, supported by difference in academic results between two types of schools, because boy and girls learn differently; a research has pointed out that boys concentrate better in a cold room whilst girls focus better in a warm environment.) An adequate range of vocabulary for the task is used, though sometimes word choice is not appropriate. The candidate makes some errors in grammar (use of articles for example) but they do not impede communication.

Sample answer: Band 7.5 score

Recently, the issue of the advantages and disadvantages of single sex and co-ed schools has become a focus of public attention. While some people hold the point of view that pupils in single sex schools perform generally better, others argue that education at mixed schools brings more advantages.

One promising aspect about single sex schools is that are renowned for academic excellence. Since boys and girls have distinctive thinking patterns and may be better suited to different learning methods, it is likely to be more effective to teach students of the same sex group rather than mixed. In addition, some studies suggested that the inclinations of children in the formative years are to gravitate towards their own sex. As a result, single sex schools provide a more natural atmosphere for the growth of pupils and contribute to better performance in their work.

Co-ed schools offer a more ideal preparation before going to university or work. Students can get along with more kinds of people and develop further their communication and negotiation skills. This kind of educational experience can also affect one's family in the future. For example, research has found that the probability of boys studied in single sex school getting divorced and suffering from depression in their 40s is considerably higher than those educated at mixed schools.

To conclude, I assume that the optimal choice would be attending mixed schools before Year 12 and transferring to a single sex school in sixth form, and that was the path I followed. Pupils would have sufficient time to get used to the environment with peers of opposite sex, whilst in a single sex sixth form college they can focus on exams and work on university application with less distraction.

Examiner commentary

The candidate addresses all parts of the task fully and presents a clear, balanced position. All ideas are extended and supported by examples. Information is organised logically and a range of cohesive devices are used appropriately, though they could have been used more clearly to signpost the topic of the penultimate paragraph. A good range of lexis is used and there are more uncommon words featured (gravitate, formative). There are only occasional grammatical and lexical mistakes but the majority of sentences are error free.

Author: Verity Cole

Publisher: Jacquie Bloese

Editor: Amanda Anderson

Designer: Andrea Lewis

Cover design: Nicolle Thomas

Picture research: Suzanne Williams

Illustration: Pages 7, 10, 11, 22, 23, 30, 31, 32, 34, 35, 38, 39, 42, 46, 47, 50, 54, 55 & 58:
Oxford Designers & Illustrators

Picture credits:
Page 12: G.Clerk, pidjoe/iStockphoto.
Page 16: P.Beavis, A.Crowley/Getty Images;
Kali9/iStockphoto.
Page 18: monkeybusinessimages/iStockphoto.
Page 20: DragonImages, kupicoo/iStockphoto.
Page 22: 4FR/iStockphoto; John Oxley Library/
State Library of Queensland.
Page 24: herraez/iStockphoto.
Page 26: J.Jacobson, marthof/iStockphoto.
Page 28: danikancil, milehightraveler, Starcevic/iStockphoto.
Page 34: M.Horwood/GC Images/Getty Images.
Page 36: S.Rawley/Alamy Stock Photo.
Page 40: D.Chard, M.Clarke/AFP, M.Tama/Bloomberg/
Getty Images; L.Steward/iStockphoto.
Page 48: B.Rindoff Petroff, T.Yu/Getty Images;
monkeybusinessimages, obas/iStockphoto.
Page 50: Bet_Noire, drbimages, PhonlamaiPhoto,
Zerzaaman/iStockphoto.
Page 52: J.Lund/iStockphoto.
Page 56: kmaassrock, RossHelen/iStockphoto.

The publishers are grateful for permission to reproduce and adapt the following copyright material:

Line graphs on page 14 and page 15 Data source:
'Child trends Databank (2014)' © Child Trends, 2014

'Apprenticeships facing an image problem as parents favour higher education for their children' by Greg Russell
© Herald & Times Group

'IELTS Writing Task 2: sample discussion essay' by IELTS Simon. Reproduced from ielts-Simon.com

'Median annual gross income of employees in different countries, in 2015 ($),' 'Senior and management positions held, in 2015 (%)' Source: Global Gender Gap Report 2015, World Economic Forum, Switzerland, 2015

'Academic IELTS Writing task 1 Sample 145 – Village of Stokeford in 1930 and 2010' IELTS Mentor (www.ielts-mentor. com). Reproduced with permission from IELTS Mentor

'Running shoe manufacture,' 'The manufacture of a skateboard' Source: www.madehow.com © Advameg, Inc.

'UK sugar intake compared to the recommended maximum of 5% energy', 'Contributors to sugar intake in the UK – children aged 4 to 18 years', 'Contributors to sugar intake in the UK – adults aged 19 to 64 years' Source: Public Health England, Sugar Reduction The evidence for action, October 2015 © Crown copyright 2015 Reproduced under the terms of the Open Government Licence v3.0

'Teen exposure to TV advertising by product type and age group', 'Trends in exposure to TV advertising for all fast food restaurants by age group' Source: Nielsen /
www.fastfoodmarketing.org/media/FastFoodFACTS_Report. pdf

'Diabetes infographic' Reproduced from www.who.int/
diabetes/global-report. © 2016 WHO

'Type 2 diabetes' Source: Diabetes – Fact Sheet No 312
Updated November 2016 © 2016 WHO

'Recorded crime against number of parks with CCTV' Source:
'The impact of CCTV: fourteen case studies' Home Office
Online Report 15/05 © Crown copyright 2005

'Changes in recorded crime in CCTV systems 2016–2018'
Data from: 'Home Office Research Study 292 Assessing the
impact of CCTV' by Martin Gill and Angela Spriggs

'Social networking usage by gender and age 2008–2015, GB'
© Institute of Practitioners in Advertising (IPA)

'Social network user percentage of population in the United
States 2015-2021' Data source: statista.com; 'Revenue from
digital advertising in the United States from 2015 to 2021'
© Statista 2016

**The publishers are grateful for permission from
Scholastic Inc., for use of the following articles and data:**

'Do you get enough sleep?' (Scholastic Math, September 1st,
2014); 'Stages of rock' (Science World, February 4th, 2013);
'The Nitrogen Cycle' (Science World, 'Taking on World Hunger
Assessment Package', October 12th, 2015).

The author would like to thank her IELTS students whose
writing experiences have inspired many of the exam skills
covered in this book and whose work is included in the
practice test sample answers.